Published by Get Sidetracked *2021*

GETsidetracked**.co**

DREA
MERS
WHO
DO

DISSENT from
business as usual

As a pioneer you see something - a possibility, an idea, a way that things could be better or new or different. And then you make something happen out of what you see. It's a gift, a call, a way of being in the world. You can't help it - it's who you are. Not everyone is a pioneer. But we need pioneers because without them we'll just get stuck with the way things are.

Pioneers dissent from business as usual.
Pioneers make a way where there is no way.
Pioneers have a gift of not fitting in.

The world is broken in so many ways.
But another world is possible.

This book is for you if you are a pioneer and you long for and dream of that better world and you want to do something about it. We don't just want dreamers; we want dreamers who do.

I have pulled together a mix of research, stories, conversations, articles, and insights from a range of pioneers who are doing it. I hope it will inspire you and give you some practical help as you use your imagination and creativity to build something out of who you are, what you see, the dissatisfaction that bugs you, the passion you carry and the talents you have as you go on an adventure of the imagination.

Jonny Baker

Written and edited by **Jonny Baker**
Design, illustrations and layout by **Jon Birch**

Published April 2021 ISBN: 978-1-8384544-0-1
Copyright GETSidetracked © 2021

Printed by **Park Communications Ltd**

CONTENTS

Build. 109

Change. 135

What have we *learned?* 176

True North. 181

What *is* pioneering?

I have asked pioneers this question before they have had a chance to learn sophisticated answers and this is what it boils down to...

Finding a new way or path

Starting and building stuff

Responding to injustice
to make a better world

Our survey said...

We asked 135 pioneers some questions.
This is what they said...

Why did you start pioneering?

Answers shown in order of preference

Which of these describes your pioneering project best?

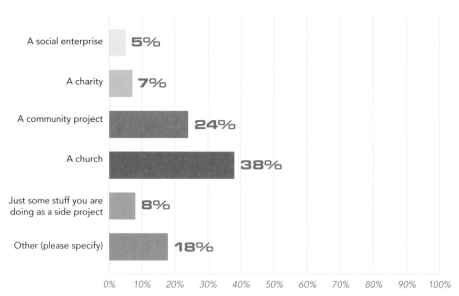

A social enterprise	5%
A charity	7%
A community project	24%
A church	38%
Just some stuff you are doing as a side project	8%
Other (please specify)	18%

How long have you been working on your pioneering project?

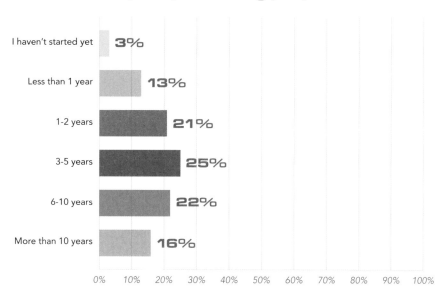

I haven't started yet	3%
Less than 1 year	13%
1-2 years	21%
3-5 years	25%
6-10 years	22%
More than 10 years	16%

Is your pioneering...

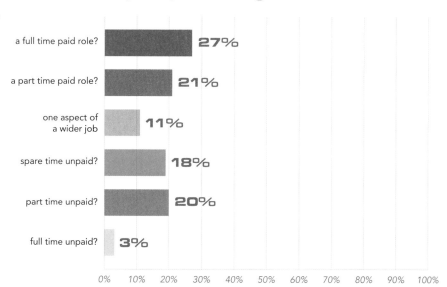

a full time paid role?	27%
a part time paid role?	21%
one aspect of a wider job	11%
spare time unpaid?	18%
part time unpaid?	20%
full time unpaid?	3%

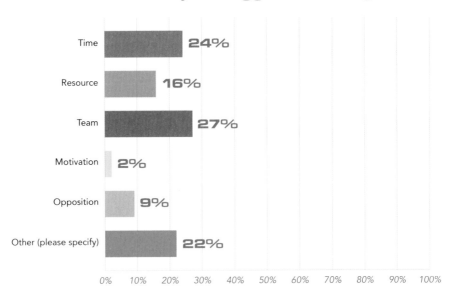

What is your biggest challenge?

Time	24%
Resource	16%
Team	27%
Motivation	2%
Opposition	9%
Other (please specify)	22%

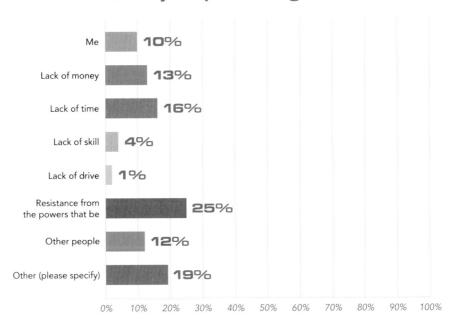

What is most likely to derail your pioneering?

Me	10%
Lack of money	13%
Lack of time	16%
Lack of skill	4%
Lack of drive	1%
Resistance from the powers that be	25%
Other people	12%
Other (please specify)	19%

Which do you value most – freedom or money?

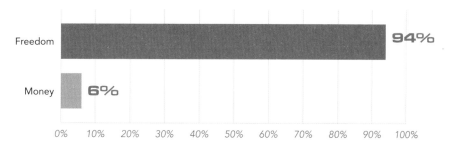

Freedom — **94%**
Money — **6%**

0% 10% 20% 30% 40% 50% 60% 70% 80% 90% 100%

What do you feel you need most help with in your pioneering?

[Top 10 with most frequently cited first]

Administration, practical and managerial skills
Support, permission and understanding at structural level
Trust by that same structure
Team – finding other like-minded people
Encouragement
Finance + funding
Finding good accompaniment, mentor, spiritual direction, or guide
Space or network for pioneers where I don't have to explain myself
Theology and training
Time

What do you know now that you wish you knew when starting out?

[Top 10 with most frequently cited first]

How hard it is with church structures/systems
It takes longer than you think
Be true to who you are – you're not crazy
You can't do it alone
It's a wonderful adventure
Learn church language games and clarify expectations
It's ok to fail
Keep your focus outwards on people in the community
Build in succession planning
You are not the saviour

Why does the world need pioneers?

[Top 10 with most frequently cited first]

They reach people who haven't heard the story of Jesus
They see and imagine new possibilities
They find new paths
They overcome stuckness
Status quo needs challenging
They respond to injustice to make a better world
They build new forms of church for people outside of church
They are able to adapt when world is changing
They build things
They imagine the future

Why does the church need pioneers?

[Top 10 with most frequently cited first]

To call the church outward in mission reminding her of her purpose
Church can be introverted, stuck, complacent, dying and doesn't like change
They see and imagine new possibilities
Old ways are not working
They go where others don't go, reach beyond fringe, break new ground
They speak with prophetic voice, challenging status quo, seeking God's direction
One size doesn't fit all so need new communities of faith
They help it adapt to changing world
They bring life and inspiration, wake it up
To reframe Jesus' story for today

Is everyone a pioneer?

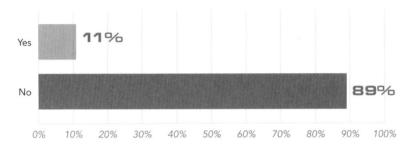

Yes **11%**

No **89%**

0% 10% 20% 30% 40% 50% 60% 70% 80% 90% 100%

Further survey results are on pages

68-69, 88-89, 116-117, 136-137

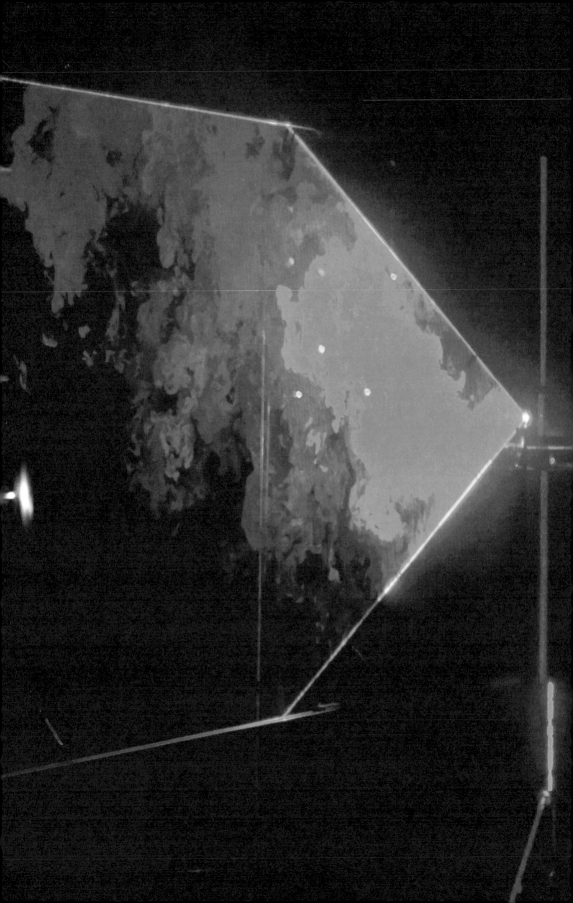

Stories →

The Good Shepherd
Boxing Community

David Harrigan is a Romford boy through and through. Having come to follow Jesus in his 20s, he wanted to work out how to connect the faith he had found which he experienced as giving him great freedom with others who had grown up in Romford. While he had learned to navigate the culture of the local Church of the Good Shepherd, he knew it was a big ask to expect people to step from their world into that. How might he do something different? He was selected to train for ordination in the Church of England as a pioneer priest and the window of three years training and a curacy gave a six year opportunity to experiment. Fast forward to year five and he has pioneered The Good Shepherd Boxing Community as he says - "church for people who want to punch stuff!"

How did you start? And why boxing?

I lived in a council residence way back when. It felt as though being there was important to us as a family and perhaps to God as well. While church was just over the road a stone's throw away, we felt more at home with the people we were living with than being in the church building. Even though I discovered the wonderful news of Jesus within the church building and with those faithful people of the church I realised the people I lived with would most likely never step across the road into that building to hear such a beautiful story of Jesus. At the same time the people I lived with knew more about what it meant

to be a community because we all lived so closely together and I always thought they could teach the church something about what this means. But still I wanted the church people to be able to step across the road so people could hear the radical news of the gospel.

People at that time, as they are now, were talking about missional communities, I wasn't even sure what they were at the time and still don't to be honest but I did know I wanted to love those people I was living with the way Christ loves them. We tried some off-the-shelf Christian resources which crashed and burned before we even got started. Plus, we didn't spend time listening we just thought we'd try something. So I wasn't too sure how we should do this but we just did what we felt was natural to us and what felt normal. There was no special formula we followed, other than we just lived and loved. Through this time, we mainly spent time hanging out just getting to know people by having beers on the stairwells, chatting and having BBQs in the communal garden. While having beers one evening I laughed with a neighbour about our younger lives and what we used to get up to. We reflected on our culture and how it had shaped us; we both found a common interest in boxing. Both being parents with young children at the time we spoke about how hard it was to get away to local gyms. I remember it like it was yesterday. He said "wouldn't it be good if we had something local like

a boxing gym?" This was the birth place or more like a magical moment. I stayed awake for most of the night wondering if God was asking me to respond to this is in some way. I then spent the rest of the next day dreaming about what this could look like. From this moment I went to the church with this idea.

Below is a timeline which tells the story of what happened from that first idea. You created it for the launch of the Boxing Club as a new community of disciples in Sept 2019 and have added a couple more steps to bring it up to date.
Can you pick one or two moments that stand out for you?

The stand out is the way they have always responded to me and faith and the way they treat each other. It's in the way they have shown me love and the way in which I watch them love each other like that of Jesus - we treat each other like a family. They show me the face of Christ each time we meet and through the words or experiences we all share together. I am always surprised by their openness towards faith and have even been told off if I shy away from speaking up about prayer or something of the sort.

But if I was pushed here are two stand outs:
Aqua Bounce. Aside from the regular boxing nights, each year we have planned four main activities:

Maundy Thursday meal, something in the summer time, something reflective near October time and a meal at Christmas. Last year we went to Aqua Bounce which is like bouncy castles on water. Never in my life had I laughed so much, nor drank so much water, as I did that day watching each of us falling all over the place slipping and sliding. This shared experience felt deeply spiritual. As my body ached that night and for the coming days I thought about discipleship. My mind took me in a boyish playfulness of 'what if sometimes discipleship can just look like fun!' It was a day that has not been forgotten, one which we all continue to laugh about today.

Boxing compline. I reimagined compline, which is form of night prayer, for the boxing lads. I created a boxing ring in the church for them to feel at home in and I really wasn't sure how this would go down. To my shock they lapped it up. You could tell at the start it felt odd to them maybe because of what we were doing or just being in the church. We had markers throughout the service sounded by a boxing bell ringing. I had been worried about time so I shortened the service just before we began. Afterwards we all had a beer and I asked them for their feedback. With beers in hand they responded with "it wasn't long enough". Whenever we do something deeper and spiritual I am always surprised how they react which has nearly always been positive.

▶

How do you grow a church in a way that these lads feel at home in it? How do you get the imagination to see things that way?

Mainly I try to build something that just makes sense to them, creating a world which they can engage with and play in. I relate it most of the time to boxing while spending time listening and learning from them, using their cultural understandings. I try as well to reframe some of the traditions of the church so that it can find home with them. Through boxing, elements of what takes place in a service are there. When we get together on a Thursday evening the idea of confession is there in punching the punch bags. If confession is unloading or lifting those mistakes/sins of life, then I think these guys do that. They bring with them their hurts/frustrations/anger with them and in some way unload this not onto another person but into the punching bag. When holding the pads for them I can tell just by how hard they are hitting what kind of day they've had. Maybe even for them this is their lament or crying out to God in a way in which words can't convey. Through this self-emptying, or kenosis if you will, something spiritual takes place, it's a discovery about themselves and furthermore a discovery about who God is. Often it is at the end of this time that we pray together allowing something new to take place within them after they have self-emptied. It is an embodied experience spiritually, more than just the mind, but it's something they feel in the flow of, rather than me trying to persuade them to believe God is real.

I don't worry so much about whether I am growing church. Yes, my ego says I would love to grow something amazing but pushing that to one side I'll let God build his kingdom thanks. Engaging with God's mission is my primary enjoyment and if through that process church takes place then great, if it doesn't then great also. Lastly I feel church grows by the guys themselves. I once made a mistake of inviting one of the guys to a service. I made the mistake of calling it church, he turned to me and said 'why would I need to go to church when I'm already in one?'. This was a wakeup call for me! So they get to shape the kind of church we are becoming; it is not an imposed format.

In terms of imagination, I watch what others are doing, steal ideas, spend time with people I trust sharing thoughts and dreams and allowing their wisdom to shape my thinking. I do a lot of waiting just holding ideas until it births itself within me or until one of the guys says something that resonates with what I have been thinking. I listen to podcasts, I read books and get different viewpoints and try to dream up ideas on how these thoughts can fit into what I am doing. And lastly I try not to do anything churchy. I spend a lot of time thinking what would the church do and then I think 'right don't do any of that'. It's almost like writing them all out on a piece of paper and then throwing it away so I can think up new ideas that are different from the church.

Where next for the community?

Who knows really, as I'm planning on only being around for the next year. My dream would be to locate to our own building. This would mean we could meet/ and train more than once a week, as well as helping the wider community for youth, schools and such like. I don't know, maybe it will all end once I go and maybe that is OK. But I would hope it would continue without me and possibly by my departure it would go beyond my dreams into someone else's and they would birth the next step.

The Good Shepherd Boxing Community timeline

Birth place
The idea of building a space, somewhere for local people to do boxing, began through building relationships within the local community.

What next?
How can we respond to what the needs of the community are to create a boxing community where we can bring boxing and spirituality together?

Dig in!
First sessions were with a very small number. Started to wonder why no one was coming. Where do we go from here - give up or keep going?

Word becoming flesh
Others started to join. The laughter and banter began with people from different backgrounds with different stories. Praying together began.

Fellowship emerges
Through prayer and friendships something changed. People we didn't even know started coming. They were sharing life and interests, inspiring and encouraging each other. What journey is God taking us on?

Boom!
We went from being a Thursday boxing session to being a community of people who look out for each other.

" There was no **special formula** we followed, other than *we just **lived** and **loved**.* **"**

In the red corner
We explored many different types of worship, from curry on Maundy Thursday to finding a way of expressing faith and worship in a way that would be meaningful for these guys, by bringing the churches traditions and boxing together inside the ring with evening prayer.

The first supper
The boxing group extends beyond boxing to the social -beers, food, friendships. Living, sharing, talking about faith and life. Where is Jesus in this?

The hunger
The guys wanted to go further, to experience all that boxing has to offer. How do we stand with them and keep them safe? These guys trust me to be in their corner. What a privilege it is to help them on their journey.

The next level
Pickwell Foundation donated seed money which enabled myself, Glenn and Mark to become professionally trained with the Hatton Training Academy.

And the new
These guys stood in my corner as I was ordained into the Church of England. I couldn't have done it without their support keeping me real. As well as one of our guys winning a belt and becoming a champion in White Collar boxing.

CLEAN *for* GOOD

Clean for Good is an ethical cleaning company in the City of London that launched in 2017. The cleaning sector is full of poorly paid and treated workers. According to the Living Wage Foundation 60% earn below a real living wage. They are hidden workers whose work is done at times when company workers rarely see them. Clean for Good is a different kind of cleaning company. As their web site puts it they want cleaners to have a life and not just a livelihood. That difference is written into their ethical commitments. The big vision is to change the cleaning sector. Tim Thorlby, the current Managing Director says "What we really want is every cleaner in Britain to be paid a living wage with terms and conditions above statutory minimum and to be treated with dignity and respect."

It is a simple but brilliant idea. I am always interested in where good ideas come from. St Andrew by the Wardrobe is a church in the City of London. Revd Guy Treweek who was the vicar there had worked in the city and knew it well and he was aware of the extreme contrasts between the high flyers and hidden workers. The church had an intern from the Centre for Theology & Community (CTC) who he commissioned to do some research into low paid workers in the parish. That was one of the things that lit the blue touch paper according to Tim Thorlby who was then part of the CTC team. It was where the conversation about cleaners began between Guy,

and Miriam, out of which Miriam suggested that perhaps good news for cleaners might look like a different kind of cleaning company. Miriam Wakefield was employed at the time as a lay pioneer missioner by St Andrew's. In a previous job she had got to know a cleaner and had heard the tough time she had had in various jobs. That cleaner's story became a driver and motivation for Miriam especially when it was hard going. She told me "We were setting this up to transform peoples' lives. So it couldn't be tokenistic. We wanted the London Living Wage and fair contracts for cleaners and we were committed to being eco-friendly with our products. They had to have holiday pay, pension, maternity pay and so on. That immediately changes peoples' lives and has done and continues to do so."

Looking back it seems obvious but it really wasn't. Tim reflects "There were loads of needs in the parish and the standard church response is to set up a charity or run a service or do a drop in cafe. But these guys dreamed up a business. The cleaners did not need charity - they needed a decent job. So they ran with that which was a crazy idea. It was about justice not charity. I hate it when people feel sorry for our cleaners. Don't feel sorry for them. They are hard working and they just want to be paid fairly and treated fairly like anyone else."

Miriam describes the challenge of getting the pro-

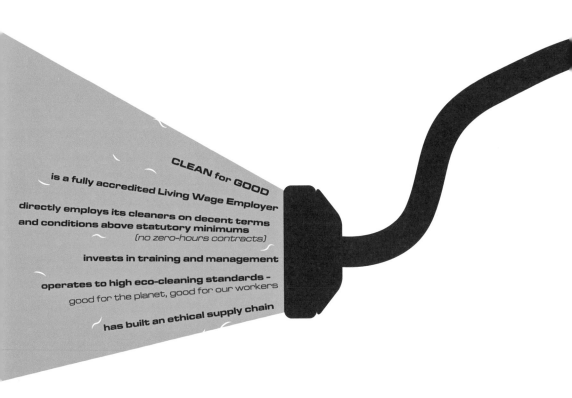

CLEAN for GOOD

is a fully accredited Living Wage Employer

directly employs its cleaners on decent terms and conditions above statutory minimums
(no zero-hours contracts)

invests in training and management

operates to high eco-cleaning standards - good for the planet, good for our workers

has built an ethical supply chain

ject going. According to Tim she was the person who provided the hutzpah, momentum and energy that said "we're bloody well going to do this!"

Miriam says, "I had no background in business at all. My degree was in youth and community work. But I have always been the sort of person that looks round to see where there is a need and seek the best solution to meet that need by discerning where God is moving and scratch that itch. It was a big itch to scratch! There was no map. We had to feel our way. That was hard but it made it interesting and exciting too. It was quite stop start which was challenging. You would have a time where lots happened and then you'd be waiting to see if you could get funding. And some of those times it was hard to see a way forward. But that meant you had to trust God and pray. That was all you could do. I always felt it would happen because it felt like God was in it. And because of that I was like - bring it on. I am fiercely determined and stubborn if I think something is of God and I'll push for it."

It took three years from idea to launch. It takes quite a bit of cost to get from being an idea to a tangible business and there is a huge amount of work to do in those years. It has to be designed and solidified and be deliverable. They managed to raise some money to do a business plan which Tim did. That began to persuade him it might work if

the numbers worked. Miriam meantime won a competition to go on Church Mission Society's (CMS) Make Good week where she worked on the vision and plan to give it shape and made what proved to be some good connections with Martin who is now Chair of the board and with CMS who became one of the investors and with Matryoshka Haus who connected the team to Catherine who became the first business manager. They worked to raise 100k of initial investment and by the time they got to 85k the board decided to press go. From the off it was a team effort. Miriam reflects "One of the key takeaways if I look back was building team and a wider network of support. I wouldn't have been able to write the business plan but Tim in particular at CTC was much better equipped to do that. I worked on the things I could do and played to my strengths. But where my weaknesses were I found other people to fill those gaps."

At the time of the launch in spring 2017, Miriam's direct involvement had stopped through maternity leave and she then moved from her job to train for ordination. Tim was chairing the Board at the time and looks back on starting the business

"It's huge uncertainty. You have a plan, hire someone, have some cheerleaders. But fundamentally you need customers so it's marketing and sales. It was serendipity (aka God) but on our first day our first customer walked in and said I need a cleaning company. They were our biggest customer and it took some work to get them on board but day one and we had a customer! I still don't know how that happened. Then it was just lots of work - web site, networking, and so on. In the early days it was largely word of mouth. But after 6 months you run out so need to be in the marketplace. Increasingly people coming through the door were people we didn't know. Year one was setting up lots of systems and processes. The end of year one I took over as Managing Director when our 'start up' manager moved on. Year two was about moving from doing cleaning to doing cleaning really well - i.e. quality. Secondly it was about growth, clarifying the message. Year three was also about growth. We are more expensive in the sector so when we tender we don't compete on price. We compete on story.

In the early days we focused on competitive prices to get customers through the door but if we continued in that vein we would not have been sustainable, so the switch to story with a higher price was an important evoluton. And interestingly the customers who come on that basis are loyal because they believe in what you are doing."

In March 2020, Clean for Good finished three years of business with around 45 cleaners employed and nearly 50 customers and made a commercial profit for the first time. They had proved that you can run a cleaning company in Central London that is commercial and also pays and treats its cleaners well! Having got to the end of March 2020 and proving it works lockdown due to coronavirus was announced. Within two weeks all but two of the customers shut their buildings. Tim reflects "That was the most stressful two weeks of my life. It was awful. Within a week it wasn't clear if we would survive. Then the government announced the furlough job retention scheme and that has saved our business. We put nearly everyone into furlough. The government scheme pays about 65% of our total costs. As a Living Wage Employer we resolved to carry on paying 100% because of our commitment to pay the London Living Wage. So we invoiced our customers for the financial gap and they have been fantastic. It was an open question whether they would pay and we had some difficult conversations with some customers, especially those suffering financial stress themselves. It's been a roller coaster. At the time of writing, Clean for Good has survived the year of Covid-19 and three Lockdowns. Most of the team have been retained through the year, and every cleaner has been paid 100% of their wages throughout. It has been a tough year, but the business has weathered the storm.

The vision remains to change the cleaning sector and every cleaner in Britain to be paid a living wage with terms and conditions above statutory minimum and to be treated with dignity and respect. Clean for Good are demonstrating that it is possible to do that and want to encourage more companies to do the same thing.

Clean for Good timeline

Nov/Dec 2013
The idea emerges that the best way of serving the contract cleaners in our parish was to establish a positive alternative business.

Spring 2014
Mapping exercise CTC completed.

Aug 2014
Dragons Den competition at Greenbelt Festival.

Nov 2014
Make Good course.

Jan/Feb 2015
Business plan begun (there were 16 versions in the end).

May 2016
board decision to give green light.

I ask both Tim and Miriam what they would want to say to pioneers starting out. Here are some of their tips:

Start with the things you enjoy doing - where your strengths are.

An idea only deserves to succeed if it's a good idea that meets a real need - *be ruthless about the idea.*

Get some building blocks in place to show the vision and find people to fill gaps. *Build team.*

Do the maths.

Don't be afraid to ask for help. *It's easier to ask for help for a project that you believe in passionately.*

It involves sacrifice and pain - *satisfaction comes from knowing you are doing it because it is right.*

Trust God.

Feb 2017
First Business Manager
Catherine Pearson
employed.

Oct 2017
Public launch.

Feb 2018
Tim Thorlby appointed
Managing Director.

March 2020
end of three years
operating and reach
break even for first time.

**Lockdown due to
coronavirus begins**
Clean for Good
furlough most staff.

JESUS *at the* UPPER ROOM
Kim Brown

Kim Brown and some friends felt a tug of their heart strings for those at the edges in Cirencester. This led to a 20 year adventure setting up and leading the Upper Room, a drop in and community on Cirencester Market Place. Kim has recently handed on the leadership.

Jesus at supper with friends
In the late 90s, I attended a weekly Bible study with friends, women of various generations. We saw a dissonance between Jesus and his everyday encounters with people who suffered and how our churches behaved. We wanted there to be somewhere that people who were desperate, outcast or despairing could come and be welcomed, eat and pray together, find the easy love and grace of Jesus for themselves that restores and resurrects. We had an itch, a dissatisfaction, and a vision of the Kingdom and what it could look like for people who were excluded in our town. After prayer and pondering, we took courage and started to work towards creating it.

He took bread
It was scary to take hold of the idea and stick our heads above the parapet, None of our churches would support the idea and we had to deal with patriarchy and opposition. We lost some people along the way. It was costly and painful. It took eight years to get it up and running from the initial

dream – that's longer than an elephant's pregnancy! Perseverance and determination are the fuel of the pioneering journey, a stubborn tenacity to pursue a God-inspired dream and breathe it into being, fight it into being, pray it into being.

In my experience of pioneering, God calls and then expects us to put the legwork into unpacking it. That legwork included identifying the knowledge and skills we'd need, studying and seeking out others with experience and wisdom. We visited 24/7 prayer rooms. I worked at social services for a year. We started a Home-Start Scheme to support families in need and raised 150k for it. We worked to get charity status. We identified an upstairs space in a building on Cirencester Market Place, an upper room and at that stage had no paid staff and were funding the rent ourselves. It was eye opening to learn how many people felt adrift in our small town, and also how many people did not want that truth to be told.

He gave thanks
When we opened the doors of The Upper Room, we gave thanks that God had led us on the long journey. People started coming as soon as we opened the twice weekly Drop-In and received support and prayer, mutually offering the same in welcome to others who came through the door. We grew and developed new services and activities in response

"It took **8 years** to get it up and running from the initial dream – *that's longer than an* **elephant's pregnancy!**"

to need. New groups of people began to come with new needs; news spread through word of mouth, we never advertised. We supported single parents, men who were homeless, people experiencing mental illness, people with disabilities and others who had experienced abuse or been in care, young people with little formal education, and people who wanted advocacy and support with a court process.

People coming to the Drop-In began to take hold of their faith journey and I wanted to support them, to baptise, marry, and shape worship around the sacraments. So I entered a discernment process with the Church of England to be an ordained pioneer minister, and trained with CMS. We were very much shaped by the Eucharist and the welcome of Christ for all at the table. Once a year at a summer playscheme we ran, we baptised and confirmed half a dozen to a dozen people from The Upper Room until everyone had been done. We were warmly welcomed by our Bishop, Michael Perham, who got what we were trying to do. He gave us a Bishops' Mission Order which is a way to belong in the structures of the church and our time of exile from the church came to an end. One of our leaders was commissioned as a lay pioneer minister and I was ordained as a pioneer.

Not everybody wants or needs to come into the structures of a denomination and its rules, but for us

it was a time of grace and encouragement. We were glad to find people of peace and a framework and resources to challenge us and to push against; the constraints shaped us in creative ways. Archbishop Rowan Williams visited us and this was a highlight for many of our folks in feeling seen and accepted.

He broke it
After some years of being reactive, we began to develop structures and systems, building a new team of trustees and employing staff for the first time. It was hard to say goodbye to our organic way of working but we needed to develop safer working practices, to fundraise and manage money to support our staff. I'm reminded of Jesus' saying about the grain of wheat that must fall to the ground and die – over the years practices evolved and changed repeatedly in response to the people coming along. The initial few who had started it had to die to our own preference or plan so that the initial seed could continue to produce fruit. For our mutual wellbeing, we had to be willing to keep being broken and reset, to give up power as quickly as we laid hold of it. Being a pioneer asks us to accept a lot of deaths; of ourselves, our ideas, self-determination and plans, in order to follow the wild goose chase of God.

He gave it to them
Over time, we moved to communal ways of decision making and worshipping together.

We developed our own Lectio Divina where someone leading worship would read out a passage two or three times to someone else helping to prepare. The helper would share their thoughts and hunches about what the passage might have to say to us at the Upper Room and the leader would write down what the helper had said. They would read it back and see if it felt like a fair shout and if so, the helper would share it with the group in the service. At the monthly Eucharist, the Bible passage would be divided up and read by several people; the prayers would be written by someone else, and the bread and wine would be distributed by two more people. Others would help prepare or clear away the lunch that followed. We were asked to speak at conferences about the way we worked together, and people who were timid grew in confidence and stature, speaking into a microphone in crowded conference halls. Everyone used their gifts in the way they wanted to. It was a shared ownership that led everyone to walk taller.

People had gifts, talents and ambitions that they had simply not had the opportunity to explore and asked for an Intern scheme to address this. Online courses with support and mentoring were offered and people chose to explore career development, leadership, and faith and values, finding opportunities to gain experience and practice their skills. Four young people graduated and completed two courses each, and a second phase started for others who wanted to develop skills in IT.

It was around then that I began to sense that the time had come for me to hand over the leadership fully and resign so a new way of working could evolve again. People never really feel ready for leadership, but we'd seen people grow into new roles quickly. I needed to make a clean break so people would fully pick up leadership and run with it, so I arranged a three-month handover period and divided the work up. It allowed us to resolve longstanding funding problems too. Pioneering asks us to follow the wind of the Spirit closely, paying attention and being as ready to relinquish as we were to pick up the call.
It was very hard to let go and I couldn't think straight for a while after. It has blessed and broken me in equal measure and I bear the scars of the breaking and the dying. But when I look back and see what we've done together and how we've done it, I'm proud of the ethos, the process and the people, and so thankful to God for the call and the adventure.
The Upper Room has now relocated to a ground floor space in the town centre sharing a building with the Salvation Army. This pivot helps for people wth mobility issues and is a better deal all round.

Upper Room timeline

£150

1998-2000
Bible study, prayer, walking in town, meeting people in need.

2000 & 2001
Dream about a centre.

2002 - 2004
Explore, talk, gather people for prayer.

2005
Kim works at social services for a year.

2006
Raise 150k to open a franchise of a Home-Start scheme in town.

2011
Get charity status & first trustee board. Gather team to explore opening a Foodbank in town to respond to need.

2012
Starts studying at CMS. Foodbank opens. Rowan Williams visits. Street Pastors starts up in town & uses UR as a base. Mental health team refers people to us for recovery .

2013
Get BMO from Bishop, first one in Diocese. Partner with parents to start a summer playscheme on an estate.

2014
Hire two more part time paid staff.

2015
Start allotment garde & forest spirituality. GPs in town socially prescribe & send people to us. Kim works at UR as C

*"None of our churches would support the idea and we had to deal with **patriarchy** and **opposition.**"*

*"I'm so... **thankful** to **God** for the **call** and the **adventure.**"*

2007
Visit 24/7 prayer rooms, boiler rooms & healing rooms all over UK.

2007
Find building for UR, took a year to sign the lease / we sold our house to fund it.

2008
Move into building & open in April. Ran drop in twice a week.

2009
Kim studies theology on 2 year part time course & enters discernment for CofE ministry.

2010
Initial volunteer staff leave & hire first paid part time support worker.

2016
Change of part time staff. Commission lay pioneer minister & start up a cooking group.

2017
Start intern scheme with four interns. New trustee board appointed.

2018
BMO made permanent by new Bishop. Intern takes responsibility for summer playscheme.

2019
Interns graduate. Identify two new co-leaders & hand over. Kim leaves.

2020
Next phase of intern programme starts.

Home Cafe

Meg Fry is the founder of Home Cafe in Earlsfield. She was a retail manager but felt a disparity between who she felt God was calling her to be and what she was doing. Her family moved to join an intentional community Earlsfield Friary in SW London and that began a process of working out who she was and what she was about. She quit her job with a new sense that her life's calling was to repurpose places, spaces, and people. Then that developed into a vision for a space big enough to host a community cafe that could support all sorts of other community endeavours, social action and events but in a way that was accessible for all, not just those with disposable income. Home Cafe on Earlsfield High St housed in St Andrew's church is the result.

It must be challenging to have set up a business and got it on its feet and then everything gets shut down because of coronavirus. What's been happening in lockdown?
The week before lockdown we were saying 'Ok, we're still here, still open' but quickly realised that wasn't going to be possible so we made a decision to shut and cook up the stock we had left and distribute it to schools, food banks and vulnerable people. We did that and quickly realised that there were a lot of people who would need feeding during this time. There is an Earlsfield Together network which we are involved in and so offered ourselves as a place that could create and distribute meals. Initially we used cafe funding and donations but then applied for and received grants. We have collaborated with the food bank which moved to

St Andrew's because it is bigger and it currently looks like a warehouse. We are feeding roughly 120 families and individuals a week. Most of it is done by volunteers and I am managing to pay our chef who thought he would have to find work elsewhere but has been able to stay and is passionate about what we are doing. We have a couple of furloughed chefs who are volunteering too. I have tried to protect the team as much as I can especially our low income people.

How do you see what you are doing now in relation to your initial vision?
I feel like the last three years have been preparation for this moment. We have more community engagement with the people we wanted to build community with than we ever have done before. Through the cafe we had got to know lots of people in our community but the question was always how we reach that deeper layer who aren't likely to engage with our cafe. We have been delivering to vulnerable and struggling people for five weeks now and have built really good relationships at least with some and are starting to talk about how we might support them in the future. We will hopefully become a charity to enable that. We'd like to be able to transition so we don't have to generate the income from the cafe to do this other sort of work. We don't yet know what it looks like. It could be one day a week done differently, a pay what you feel day or offering cooking lessons for a family on a low budget because some of the people we are cooking for can't cook. We are wondering about launching a cookbook of the recipes we have cooked (which has

"...we had this fear that we had built this thing and what if no one actually cares?!"

"We nailed customer service early on
which we had to!"

been like Ready Steady Cook!) interspersed with postcards from the people we have been feeding to combine our story with their stories.

That sounds amazing that so much that's creative has come out of having to close the cafe! Can we go back to the launch which was October 2017. Tell me about the early months.

It was terrifying. I remember being so excited about building the cafe, ordering the stock, doing barista training. Then the week up to launch I was having serious anxiety and dreams about no one coming in or loads of people coming and not having enough stock. I had never run a food business so we were learning as we went. We nailed customer service early on which we had to! But we had this fear that we had built this thing and what if no one actually cares?! However we were really well received. It started with mates coming in and then it was people we didn't know and now it's 90% people we didn't know. That has been lovely. When we shut our doors we had so much support from the local community. We even had one woman offering to pay our salaries for the duration to keep us being able to come back. You realise that some of the relationships we have built are really long lasting and go quite deep and we have become a real safe space for people as well as just being a cafe. It has become community hub.

On the business side did it work as you hoped, the money flows?

We have never had to apply for grant funding until now. Initially we predicted two years in we would

have to register for VAT but went over that threshold after eight months. That's been tough because all the profit goes on VAT but we have broken even every year. There's nothing left over but it's sustainable. I did the cooking for the first two years which was hard work but we have now taken John on as a chef which been incredible. He has owned that side of things and become my right hand man and is business minded and savvy. That has freed me to focus on the community side of things. We have run loads of stuff over the last two years.

What sorts of things?

We run after school stuff like lego club which is very informal, coffee mornings, perinatal groups, death cafes, elderly peoples lunch clubs. We run a big Christmas meal for the elderly people and they love that and start asking in the summer when that is going to be. We offer the space to people to come and use and do something of value in it and support us by buying coffee. We have a premium supper club that you pay for, then the profits go to running the same meal for refugees and asylum seekers for free and you are served by the people who paid for it. They have been incredible and we've worked with other refugee charities on that. We have hosted Migrateful cookery courses - they are a charity that empower refugees to teach cookery from their home countries so they've used our space. We have run beer and carols and community meals working with the Friary once a month. We also do a lot of stuff around special needs. We have some special needs schools whose kids do work experience with us for example.

How has it been with the church?

We straddle this space where we have a relationship with church and with community who view what we do differently. I was fearful that the community wouldn't come because it was in a church and also would the church interfere? We've not had that though. Our vicar Jonathan is happy to let us crack on and is very supportive. Lots of the church members love it and some volunteer with us. The community seem to come and realise there is no pressure about religion so they relax and enjoy the space. They often say there is something special about the space. It's had an effect on the team. There are so many times now where we have needed things and they have come through. I know that's God. The team aren't church goers but they notice that we are provided for. It's so tangible they are sort of naming it! It's also connected to the Friary in that it's a project the Friary launched. It wouldn't be here without them.

What would you say to people who are at a stage of dreaming about a project or the start stage?

You have to hold something but hold it lightly be-cause you have to adapt and evolve. You have to let go of your own fixed ideas. When you allow God to be in charge you have to be open to that change and adapting. Failure is how you learn. Allow people to help you - I didn't let people help me enough and was almost crushed as a result. Three years on I know now that it is established enough now that it would continue if I was taken out of the picture. It is a lot of fun - I love going in every day. There's nowhere else I would want to be. I am really happy and amazing stories come out of this.

What sort of things?

When the doors shut there was a flood of outpouring of what it meant to people which was overwhelming. I spoke to a woman who said she felt safe with a young baby in a way she didn't anywhere else because if anything happened or she needed help she knew we'd be there and help and had become friends. There was a homeless lady who slept on the pew in the church and we'd give her food. She stopped coming in after two weeks and we were a bit worried. But the following week a woman came in who looked so different and it was her back on her feet. She said God had his hand on her and being able to be in this space gave her the resilience and strength she needed to get back on

---

Home Cafe timeline

Summer 2014
Left Ikea and full time employment with a vision to set up a community cafe.

Sept 2014
Started CMS year pioneer training.

Nov 2014
Mission Entrepreneurship CMS at Pickwell.

Jan 2015
Clear plan of community cafe.

Jan 2015 - Jan 2017
Pitching to church PCC and DAC to get plann to put cafe in.

Jan 2017 - Apr 2017
Funding comes through for cafe from various donors.

Apr 2017
DAC agree plans and building work starts.

23rd Oct 2017
CAFE OPENS!

Christmas 2017
Cafe established as local hub and increasingly busy, first couple of big events.

2018
Cafe continues to esta itself. Big events inclue Just Supper Clubs and Just Sharing refugee n Amos Trust evening. Classes for adults and Home Cafe Big Lunch event at local estate. Elderly peoples lunch (Lord Dubs visits - still best highlight!)

her feet again and sort herself out. It's been humbling to be part of those sorts of things. Amazing stories of volunteers, provision, stories of change. Lots of stories!

What is the flow between the cafe, the church, the Friary?

The Friary have started the All Sorts new look monthly family service. A lot of the cafe customers come to that, a lot of families. The church has noticed an increase in baptisms. A lot of that has been through the cafe space I think! We have a couple of new members in the Friary who have come through links with the church. The cafe has created what feels like a base for the Friary too. We had 90 people at the last community meal so we are blurring the edges which is great.

How hard is it getting something going in the early stages?

The first six months were really tough and completely exhausting. The Friary always stepped in to support and friends helped me find more balance with work/family life. I definitely have a lot more balance now. The kids are part of what we do though and they hang out there after school with other friends. When it came to the dreaming and planning phase I realised it was bigger than I thought so signed up for some training for a year in pioneering with CMS to find a language for what I was talking about and I did a course on entrepreneurship

as part of that to try and figure out business and how to make it profitable. And then I just started talking to local people about what they wanted and a plan began to take shape. It was difficult finding a venue but then we thought about using the church and that came together though it took a while. I developed a business model. I talked to investors. We laid the groundwork of what we would do and how we would do it. The church signed off on it which was amazing. We then started to talk to the diocese to seek building planning permission for it, and that took a year and a half as well. I spoke to my husband Alex about him doing the building work at cost. We were keen on repurposing and re-using what we'd already got. Rather than looking at need all the time, we learned to focus on the assets we had - people, skills, investors. We also felt strongly that as a family we wanted to invest in the project, so if we were asking other people to invest we needed to do that. So we remortgaged our house and put up some money and then could say to others, "Right. We've put money in the pot. Who else wants to?" I thought that would be the hardest part. Amazingly, we managed to fund-raise all of the money within about a month and a half, and that was only £100,000. And that was only three or four trusts that gave me that money. Incredibly, we went into the project with no overheads. It's all gift, which is phenomenal. I've learned that if God wants it to happen it happens, and really you have to do very little other than stop trying to control it.

2019
Loads of supper clubs. Loads of friary events. Green Party event with Jonathan Bartley. External catering at local art fair.

Aug 2019
John Magee (Chef), comes on board and takes over food side of business and takes cafe to next level!

Feb 2020
Cafe hits profit and starts planning next steps.

Mar 2020
COVID hits. Cafe closes and partners with Foodbank and St Andrews to become a food hub looking after local folk who need food. Set up a system of free, hot and nutritious meals delivered daily. Received grant funding to do this. At peak doing 800 meals a week to local residents, homeless shelters, refugee families in our network, women's refuge centers, hospitals etc...

Aug 2020
Hit 10,000 meal mark on Aug 12th. Food hub takes a break for two weeks with a view to the cafe re-opening in September and continuing partnership with foodbank to create a community day of hospitality and wrap around care, to continue to support those we got to know during covid.

MISSIO
AFRICANUS

Harvey Kwiyani felt called at a young age and came from Malawi to serve God in mission in Europe. He arrived in Switzerland twenty years ago and has been on a journey to reflect on how Africans and other non-Western Christians engage in mission in the diaspora, among their Western neighbours. He pioneered Missio Africanus as a result.

What is Missio Africanus?

Mission Africanus is a cross-cultural mission training initiative and organisation that focuses on training African and other non-European Christians coming from the majority world trying to figure out how to engage Europe in mission.

How did it start?

Back in 2014, I worked with a group of pastors from the Redeemed Christian Church of God, a Nigerian denomination, seeking to develop a cross-cultural mission approach. It became quickly clear to me that sort of training was needed beyond just that group. No one was providing anything similar. In response, I created a space where African Christians and British Christians could get together around the question of cross-cultural ministry and multicultural church. We've expanded the vision now to include Latin Americans and Asians.

You say no one was doing that. There are obviously lots of African churches who have grown fast and are doing training. So, what is different or unique about what you do?

There are many African churches in the UK. It's fair to say they are growing because they are reaching other Africans - growth by migration. As long as there is migration from African to the UK, such churches will grow. Of course, that means as long as they can grow without doing cross cultural ministry, and should migration trends change, they stop growing. What we try to do in Missio Africanus is to teach them there is a better way to grow that is missional and faithful to their calling to engage cross-culturally with all their neighbours.

I am interested in your own story and how you came to see this gap or opportunity?

I was convinced back when I started Missio Africanus, just as I am today, that God's mission must include all Christians living in Europe, many of whom have come from Africa, Asia, and Latin America. And I was perplexed that the empowerment of non-Western Christians for mission in Europe did not feature greatly in many mission training institutions. Actually, for me, it all stared in St Gallen in Switzerland the I saw African churches thriving in what seemed to be a spiritual desert to me, yet,

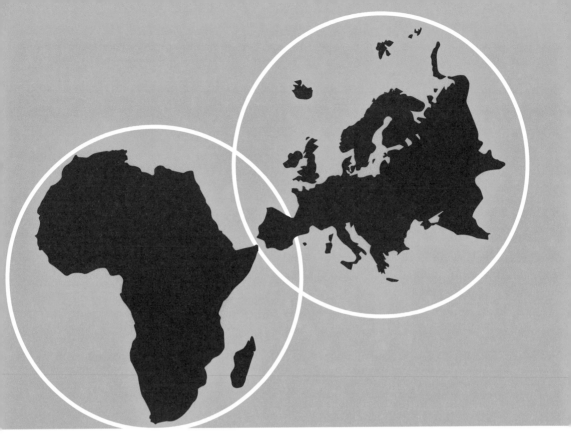

being unable to reach their European neighbours. If these migrant Christians will follow God in God's mission in Europe, they certainly need some training to learn new skills for sharing the Gospel with Europeans. Missio Africanus was established to begin to meet that need.

You seem at home in the Western postmodern culture and within African cultures. You are able to surf both worlds which seems to have been key in enabling you to innovate in the way you have.

That is due to my training. I was educated by Westerners, asking Western questions on mission in the Western world. I studied the works of people like Lesslie Newbigin here in the UK. And when I studied in the US, I was part of the Missional Church conversation. So, I came to be at home in that world even though I always felt like there was something missing – the African perspective of mission in the West. I decided to curve space for myself as an African wrestling with the question of evangelizing Westerners. And, as life would have it, I teach African theology. Thus, I now inhabit this place between African theology and Western missiology, and I am at home in both those worlds.

How does the word pioneer fit or not for you?

From Malawi the word works alright - doing some-

thing fresh at the margins, breaking new ground. In America it is associated with colonialism and the white Europeans who caused havoc and established white rule. So, it's complicated but it's not a word that bothers me. I believe that it is possible to pioneer without colonizing.

Your vision and writing advocates for a multicultural approach. Can you say more about that vision?

The Sunday morning segregation that continues in the body of Christ is not the right way to go about being church. God's gifts to the body are spread around the world but they are for nourishment of the entire body. Life in the body depends on the exchange between the parts (Eph 4:16). Here in the UK, we are lucky that we have so many parts living together in the same cities much more than other parts of the world. Those parts bring gifts for each another. Yet, monocultural churches make the exchange difficult. If we are going to really do what the body needs and keep it healthy, we have to find ways to meet together and normalise the exchange of gifts God has given us in our different cultural expressions of Christianity

How did Missio Africanus get off the ground? The early stages are often challenging.

▶

I was lucky in that I had good friends who had experience in starting things up. One was Gabriel Diya (who suddenly passed away in 2019). We initially set up a limited company but then realized that what we needed was a charity. Another friend, David Jones, was very helpful to walk us through the registration process. We started out with four key strategic priorities; congregational training, an annual conference, a journal and research. All those have worked well for six years now.

Can you share some examples of where people engage in this cross-cultural imagining how it affects their practice?

There are many. As a result of our training, Pastor Joseph Omoragbon of the RCCG in South Shields set up a football tournament for primary schools as a way of engaging in his neighbourhood in a contextually relevant manner. That tournament has brought his church closer to the communities in which they are located, thereby making their witness more visible.

There is also Joseph Ola with whom we have worked for a few years now. Our training has empowered him to lead his global online congregation

of around 3000 young people who engage with materials he is putting out every week.

On the congregational front, Pastor Dupe Adefala's congregation, Word Fountain Church in Oxford changed aspects of their evangelism strategy in response to engaging our Missional Empowerment Training program. For example, they stopped relying on sending out flyers and doing Saturday evangelism on the High Street. Instead, they started to focus on their communities' third places - places where people hang out to connect and belong and that led to grow the church differently.

How has George Floyd's murder and the heightened awareness of racism affected things?

I think that it highlights the need for us to begin to talk to one another cross culturally in an intentional manner. Racism has always been an issue. George Floyd made it easier to see and agree that we have a problem. So, what do we do about it? The best way to begin to move forward is to really engage in cross-cultural conversations like this, to see one another and recognise the presence of one another much better. That allows us on one hand not to be colour blind and on the other to answer each other's questions.

"The best way to begin to move forward is to really engage in cross-cultural conversations like this..."

Cherish

Following a career in retail management, Erika Biscoe trained as a nail technician. She and her husband Ian got involved in church planting and Erika sensed a call to be ordained as a pioneer minister with the unique idea of combining manicures with her ministry.

What is Cherish?

Cherish is a six-week course or journey for teenage girls looking at contemporary life issues they face - anxiety, depression, eating disorders, dreams, goals, relationships, finding your own voice, self harming, self worth. All the things they are bombarded with through contemporary culture . We teach them how to do a basic manicure doing a section each week until they can do a full one by the end. We weave the story of Esther through the whole course. Her story has resonated with me for years and has all the issues and themes in terms of what she went through. Each week has three sections - the manicure, someone shares their story and then we look at Esther and a theme or issue and have discussion in groups. It's a sensitive course so confidentiality is important. They get lovely materials, journals, a bottle of nail varnish each week with a word like cherish on and a verse from the bible to encourage them. The final week they get a manicure kit and we encourage them to bless others with their new skill.

What was the spark that started Cherish?

We were involved in a church plant near Bicester, Oxfordshire and felt doing kids church was a good thing to start with. At the end of the session the boys went to play football and I took my nail stuff for the girls and it was huge success. We then moved to an existing church plant in Bicester town and it was here that I then started offering free manicures. Those conversations were just really easy - it flowed into faith stuff and we'd share our stories. In my own mind I had linked the story of Esther with offering manicures and my original idea was Esther's Nail Spa - a comfortable welcoming space to come in and have a chat and have a nice experience while having your nails done. Around that time I felt called to explore ordination and trained with CMS. One of the modules was a mission entrepreneurship week where I brought the idea and it was in that week that the thought of a course for girls emerged. I had already done manicures with girls at the youth group at Emmanuel Church where I was and got into some really deep conversation about anxiety, depression, suicidal thoughts and so on. I had to do a pitch at the end of the week which was terrifying but I came away believing this could really happen. I then had conversations with others when I got back, sat down and worked on it and Cherish was born. I ran the first course

in June 2013 with girls from the youth group six months later.

Why is this your passion? Why these themes with girls?

When I was 15 I was in a desperate place because I was pregnant. I had a termination. Two weeks after I was back at school sitting exams and we never talked about it at home. My parents had taken over and now it was like 'move on', but of course I couldn't move on because I had experienced trauma and didn't know how to cope with that. I lost my self worth and confidence and was in a bad state. I had recently become a Christian through my RE teacher and I think if I hadn't my life could have taken a very different turn. Once I had gone through many years of shame and dealing with it (not that I think you ever fully deal with it) I sensed God would want me to share it and walk alongside others who have had that experience or similar. It's a hidden scar within. That's why my heart is for girls facing these kinds of issues.

That's a powerful story and I can totally see how this fits for you. Is it just you involved or is there a team?

I built up a team. They came from me talking about the vision. I have a beauty therapist, a graphic designer, a counsellor and coach on the team. They were in my church which is incredible really. I looked for people with particular skills that we needed and I didn't have. It actually wasn't hard to gather the team. We meet weekly for an hour to keep the connection and sense of team.

How has it developed since that pilot course?

We did the design and branding for that initial course and that has stayed but we have tweaked and developed the kit trying out various things. We ran it in primary schools, secondary schools, at a youth morning, ladies breakfasts and so on. I was then asked by a youth worker if she could run it and so trained her, she raised money for the kits which we put together as a resource. That was run in London with their youth group. So at that point we realised it could work with others and be a resource. I then thought I should run a training day for trainers to be able to share the passion and ethos of it rather than just pass on the product as it's about relationships. I kept that to 9 people with the plan that they could then buy kits and run courses. But that was this year before lockdown due to Covid 19 so that has stopped them running it but i am sure they will. In lockdown I have run it for a group online, delivering kits and nail varnish to their homes.

▶

That has worked surprisingly well and has meant we have recorded videos of talks and so on.

How does the money add up?

I have always wanted girls to be able to do it for free so we raised money initially through a grant from the diocese outreach fund and from individuals. I have recently applied and received a grant of 30k to develop it further. This includes some money for admin, kits and so on. I have someone else who does the numbers which is good because it is not my forte but we do have a spreadsheet now mapping ins and outs for course materials, the resource kit, training, and branded products which we plan to make and sell. That is mapped out over the next two years in a business plan. We have been given a lot by the team in terms of time and the graphic design done for free for example. At the moment the accounting is run under the church's umbrella. The next step is finishing the web site and I hope to set it up as a charity in its own right but we're not there yet. I have also run it with Mums in the cafe so we have realised these issues are not just relevant for teenagers.

Do you have ongoing contact with those who do the course?

Where it is in a youth group there is an ongoing community they are part of. But that's harder in schools. In some cases we have offered mentoring or coaching where it seems there is a need for more but it's not always possible.

What difference does it make in the girls lives?

We get feedback on all sessions and at the end of the course. That's encouraging - they say it gives them confidence, inspiration, they don't feel alone, there are particular stories that move them that they resonate with, it gives them tools to manage and control things when issues arise. The youth worker said she found it really broke something open with the girls because of the level of openness and honesty and allowed them to get into deeper issues.

Do you still dream of Esther's Nail Spa?

I do still dream. I'd love to have a VW van that could be a pop up nail bar and gin bar at festivals, but we'll see.

Cherish timeline

1992
Trained as a nail technician.

1999
Sheffield, inspired by story of Esther.

2002
Moved to Heyford Park to church plant.

2008
Started Kidz church and conversations reminded me of the book of Esther and had idea of Esther's nail bar.
Calling to Pioneer ministry.

2010
Moved to Emmanuel Bicester .

2011
Set up a café in Emmanuel and offered free manicures.

Cherish is a six-week course or journey for teenage girls looking at contemporary life issues they face...

anxiety, depression, eating disorders, dreams, goals, relationships, finding your own voice, self harming, self worth...

All the things they are bombarded with through contemporary culture.

2012
Trained as a Pioneer with CMS.

2013
Worked with youth, touched by conversations. Missional Entrepreneurship week Pickwell Manor.

2014
Ran the first Cherish course with the youth group girls.

2015
Ordained.

2015-20
Ran courses in youth groups, local secondary school, pamper day, ladies' breakfast, primary school, piloted as resource with St Andrews Fulham.

Feb 2020
Training trainers day.

The SACRED BEAN

Jo Howie is a pioneer in Derby doing a job share with her husband Darren. Sacred Bean is an enterprise that has grown out of their pioneering.

Sacred Bean started as just a hobby. Darren and I both love good coffee but for Darren, coffee is more of an obsession. He bought a hand roaster and started roasting his own beans on our kitchen table at night after the kids were in bed. At the time, Darren was doing a Pioneer Curacy in Derby City Centre and as part of it, was running a mentoring project for ex-offenders. He thought that he could roast with some of the guys on the project as a kind of discipleship tool.

Very quickly, people started to ask us if they could buy the coffee so we started to sell in really small quantities. It became obvious pretty early on that this could be something bigger. Both Darren and I are really passionate about helping people with barriers to employment, such as previous offences or those recovering from addiction, gain skills and experience to help them turn their lives around.

Shortly before Darren's curacy came to an end, we purchased a bigger (1kg) roaster and it was temporarily housed in the church chancel. Darren and I were offered a job share as Pioneer Missioners to the city for Derby Methodist Circuit and it was at this time that we started thinking more seriously about the future of Sacred Bean, although I am not sure it even had a name by that point!

We decided to create a CIC (community interest company) and we joined forces with two friends, Chandra and Tim to be the four directors. Chandra is great at all the nitty gritty details like policies and grant applications, and Tim is the money man. Thankfully, the Methodist Circuit really saw the potential and value in what Sacred Bean was doing and agreed to let us run it from Susanna Wesley House. SWH is next door to the house where we live on a new housing development in Derby city centre, we run it as part of our jobs and it is a sort of mission, hospitality, retreat, community space all in one.

So Sacred Bean is a coffee roasting business and we sell really great artisan coffee. However, it's not just about the coffee, it's also about the people. We want to give people hope, and provide people with opportunities to gain employment as well as welcoming them into community. Sacred Bean not only teaches people how to roast coffee, we are also able to teach people barista skills, as well as things like sales, customer service and marketing. Some of

Jo Howie

the people who have trained through Sacred Bean have already gained a qualification in roasting.

Before coronavirus, we were roasting weekly out of Susanna Wesley House and we usually work with approximately five or six people at any one time. There's a real sense of community forming around Sacred Bean and Friday became a kind of community day, with a shared lunch, an act of worship and there were always lots of people in and out, not just the trainees, but people from the local community, others with links to Sacred Bean, people from different churches. People are always welcome to come and see what we do.

As part of my studies at CMS, I wrote a Coffee 'Eucharist' for this Sacred Bean community day and Darren leads it every week during lunch. It has meant something to those involved with Sacred Bean because it is relevant to their story and what they are doing.

We continued to roast during coronavirus and our orders increased, although we couldn't work with all of the trainees in person.

We are outgrowing our 1kg roaster and our room at Susanna Wesley House and so Sacred Bean will be moving to a new home in the not too distant future. I put forward a proposal to re-purpose a disused Methodist Church and that has been approved, so Sacred Bean's Roastery will occupy the building along with an artisan coffee shop, offices and a community space. We are looking forward to the future.

The biggest problem has just been keeping on top of demand, it has grown quicker than we've really been ready for and we don't want to lose focus from the purpose of Sacred Bean, which is the people. It has been a bit Catch 22 - we need to expand to be able to create employment opportunities but in order to do that, we need more resources. We have been approached to supply coffee shops and we hope to be able to do that in the future but at the moment it's one step at a time.

The best thing is seeing people thrive doing something they enjoy. We had a wonderful day where we opened up SWH and the trainees made free speciality coffees (lattes, flat whites, etc) for people so they could practise their new skills, and we had over 70 people come in throughout the day, builders working on the development, local residents, police officers, people passing through from the train station. It was great watching the guys chat to people, talk about the coffee and just to see their passion for what they are doing shine through.

▶

The Sacred Bean
EUCHARIST

This is a table of welcome, ALL are invited to join in this special act. An act of remembrance, an act of imagination, and an act of anticipation.

The coffee bean is a bit like us humans, it needs the right environment in which to thrive. It needs to be looked after and treated well in order to reach its full potential. It needs the input of others; it needs to be handled with care.
(a bowl of coffee beans is passed around and everyone takes a bean)

Like the coffee beans you hold, all here are unique and hold so much potential. God-given potential. These beans are seeds, they represent hope. Hope to a broken world, hope in the midst of despair, hope of a future.

(hold the coffee bean in your closed fist)

For the times we have not fulfilled our potential
We are sorry God
For when we have not seen the potential that you have placed in others
We are sorry God
For when our actions have caused others to wither rather than thrive
We are sorry God

(Place beans all together in bowl)

You have called us to become one, your Holy church, to work together for the purpose of your Kingdom

(Beans are put into the grinder and then ground)

God, your word reminds us that we are all special, and like these beans, blended together to create a delicious and distinct flavour, when we join together, it is beautiful.

(The stove is lit)

Jesus, you are the light of the world. Your light empowers, inspires and guides us.

(The coffee grinds are put into the stove top and it is then put on the stove to brew)

As the coffee brews, reflect on the journey of this coffee, including those involved. From the farmer that nurtured and grew the coffee

plant and the hands that picked the beans, to those that have expertly roasted the beans. Think about and give thanks for those that have influenced your journey and nurtured you, to the point of being at this table today.

(Once the coffee is brewed)

Come Holy Spirit, come amongst us and within us, come upon this gift from creation and by your power, as it enters our bodies, help us to accept the grace that Jesus made possible

(The coffee is poured into cups and distributed to each person)

Jesus gathered at a table with friends and shared a meal.
Today, we gather as friends, to drink this coffee.

Jesus described himself as 'the bread of life', and at that table, he tore a loaf of bread, and told his friends to eat it and remember him.
At this table, there's no bread, just coffee. Coffee that provides, coffee that gives life.
As we sip this coffee, we remember that Jesus gave his life for ours
Jesus, we remember you

(sip coffee together)

On that same night, Jesus drank wine with his friends. He told them that the wine represented his precious blood, that was to pour from his body as he hung on a cross. At this table, there's no wine, just coffee. Bittersweet Coffee.
As we sip this coffee, we remember that after the bitterness of death, came the sweetness of life.
Jesus, we remember you

(sip coffee together)

After a moment's silence...

'Taste and see that the Lord is good". May the taste of this coffee lingering on your lips, remind you of God's goodness and of the richness of life. God is like the farmer who grew the beans that created this coffee, we are nurtured and loved, and although individual, our potential is fulfilled when in community with others.
Farmer God, thank you for your loving care. Give us compassion to demonstrate that same loving care to others, including those around this table.

Amen.

REVS

Cars, Community, Restoration

ADAM GOMPERTZ

The REVS project first came to life as a response to a question of how one particular church might engage with the people in its local context. That was a very affluent 'gated' neighbourhood where cars as well as houses were a way people liked to enjoy their wealth. That the Curate (that will be me) who came up with the seemingly 'different' idea of holding a classic car show just happened to be a complete petrolhead and a former car designer at least gave it some degree of credibility.

Indeed, that start of 28 cars in a church car park has now become a small network of monthly meetings happening in various locations of the West Midlands, a growing annual event that is attended by around 400 people and a social media group with over 5000 members. And it all happens because I felt called to use something that I am very passionate about (cars), to communicate something God is very passionate about; His love for people, relationship, restoration and community. That shared passion for things automotive became an area of common ground for so many people.

The inspiration and thinking behind it all came earlier, while at bible college, where it had seemed to me that life as a trainee church leader meant turning my back on all the things that I had done in my work life until then. For someone who had always wanted to be in the very competitive industry of vehicle de-

sign, I recall having a profound sense of grief during those first few months of writing theological essays. That was also the time I discovered The Shaping of Things to Come by Alan Hirsch and Michael Frost, a book which was to connect two worlds I had thought were mutually exclusive. In those pages I read the authors challenging the established church to rethink years of missional endeavour; the traditional way of inviting potential new disciples to myriad events and services was no longer working. Instead Frost and Hirsch encouraged any who would listen to go and inhabit the places where these yet-to-be disciples lived out their lives; it was the call to incarnational, missional living.

I found myself becoming excited by the realisation that perhaps my calling meant 'going out' rather than 'gathering in', that those experiences prior to my training were to be valuable in some way. This was confirmed for me by an understanding tutor who would remind me that 'God does not do waste'. REVS was the result of that thinking, praying, reading and a lot of wrestling through ideas about what being church in the world of Car Culture might look like.

There are many people who are part of that culture. According to the Federation of British Historic Vehicle Clubs last year around ten million people expressed an interest in classic vehicles, with around

*I found myself becoming excited by the realisation that perhaps my calling meant **'going out'** rather than 'gathering in'...*

three million having attended a national historic vehicle event in the previous year. The Goodwood Festival of Speed has an attendance of over 100,000 people on each of the three days it is held.

One of the catalysts for REVS to develop as a project was my own battle with mental health issues which saw me taking a break from curacy for seven months in 2015. During the recovery from my breakdown, and a subsequent move to Shropshire, I was mindful of the restorative work God was doing within me, and looking towards the future I felt it was something that many others also needed.

From that point REVS became far more than just a car show, it became an active metaphor; as someone may take time, effort, and expense to restore a classic vehicle, so too God takes the cost, time and effort to restore broken lives. I realised that an annual event is not enough when seeking to deepen relationships, and so in 2017 REVS launched a monthly breakfast meet at a roadside café just outside of Shrewsbury. REVS Shrewsbury is a regular meeting of people gathering to share their passion for their classic vehicles, to build community, and be a safe place should they want to chat about other things going on in their lives. They can even request prayer through simply, and privately, posting a request slip through the sunroof of my old car.

The following year we were approached by a team from another church in the Stourbridge area to start a second group, running along similar lines; REVS Enville had its first meeting in October 2018. Currently we are in discussion with others to start a third group outside Stoke on Trent, and possibly a fourth towards Ludlow.

Metaphorically the aim for these groups is to act like service stations on the journey of life, a place to rest and recover, before setting off again. In practice, we have seen community grow, with people feeling that the meetings act as their safe space, with an option to simply talk cars or 'go deeper'. They have also been places for me to explore a practical theology that engages with people on their terms. I liken this to becoming bilingual, talking two languages; finding those symbols, metaphors and pictures that help people move from classic cars to deeper issues of life, faith, hope, community and love. Themes of 'restoration', of being 'fearfully and wonderfully made', and 'significant journeys taken' all have a resonance on both an automotive and spiritual level. It is the simple idea of using one passion to speak in to another; nothing new when you consider how Jesus spoke of farmers sowing seeds, vines and branches, and shepherds and sheep.

With the advent of COVID 19, we, like many, have had to postpone our groups, but we have developed an online version which resulted in two 'virtual' car events where people could submit videos of their cars, share their stories, interact with others, and email prayer requests. The response was overwhelming; 'REVS Limiter' currently has an online membership of over 5200 people, and a whole team of contributors.

Looking ahead, The REVS Pilgrimage, a classic car tour of the North Wales early Christian pilgrim routes, will take place in May 2021. I also have a dream of a central REVS venue; restoring an old garage, with workshop space for hire so people can work on their own cars, a café area that could host movie nights, community events, and serve as a worship space.

There are challenges. Funding will always be an issue. I have also battled with the perception of needing to demonstrate the validity of the REVS project to others who may perceive it as 'not churchy enough' and who may try to change it accordingly, although being given a Bishops' Mission Order has, to some extent, resolved this. The loneliness of Pioneer Ministry is also something I am very aware of, so surrounding myself with a group of people who will support, challenge, pray and keep me accountable has been invaluable.

If I have learnt anything through all of this, it is that God is a whole lot bigger than we often credit Him, He is already out there at work and by his grace invites each one of us to get involved. Even a petrolhead!

REVS timeline

2014
The first REVS car show held in Little Aston - a total of 28 cars (and a result of prayer walking around a very wealthy parish wondering how God was going to open the gates of all those posh houses).

2015
The second REVS show with around 43 cars - a notable thing was the agreement of the local residents association to let us use their private road to have a column of cars on display just next to the church (something we were told would never be agreed - God is good).

2017
REVS Show moves to Shrewsbury and number goes up to around 60 cars May 2017 - the first local REVS group meeting monthly sets up just outside Shrewsbury - hence its name REVS Shrewsbury.

2018
REVS 2018 - annual show again in Shrewsbury. September - I start studying at CMS - very grateful for the community there. October the start of the second group called REVS Enville (surprisingly based at the village of Enville) . REVS also features on Songs of Praise (and some filming happens at REVS Shrewsbury).

"...service stations
on the journey of life."

2019
REVS 2019
the annual show grows to
just under 100 cars.

2020
Four virtual events held in
May, June, September, and
November for people frus-
trated with not being able
to attend car shows. Each
finishes with a prayer of
blessing. The REVS Limiter
Facebook community has
grown to over 6000 people.
REVS has won the 'Lock-
down Initiative' award at
the annual Historic Motor
Vehicle Awards, the Classic
and Sportscar award for innovative use of social media,
was a finalist for the Royal
Automobile Club awards for
'Motoring Spectacle'.

2021
In 2021 won the Guild of
Motoring Writers award for
'Special Contribution to
Motoring'.

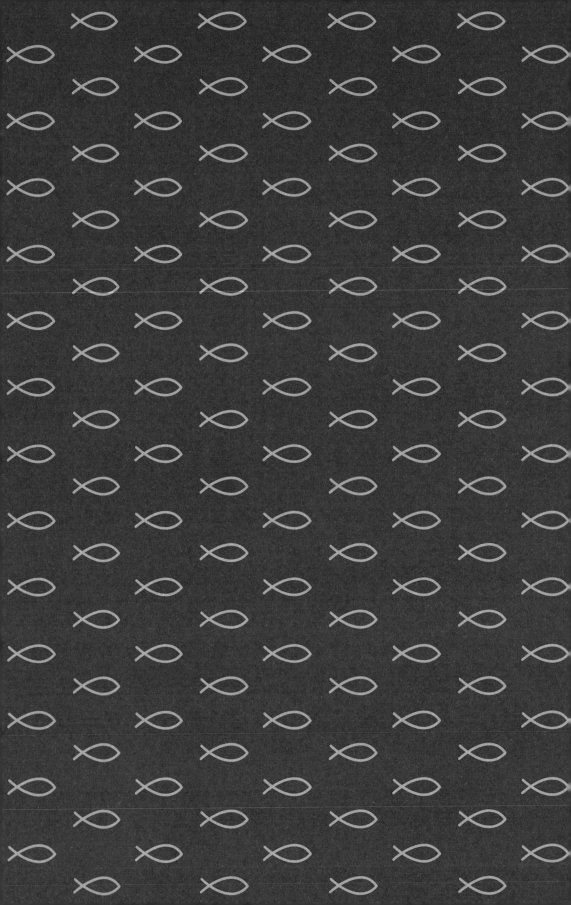

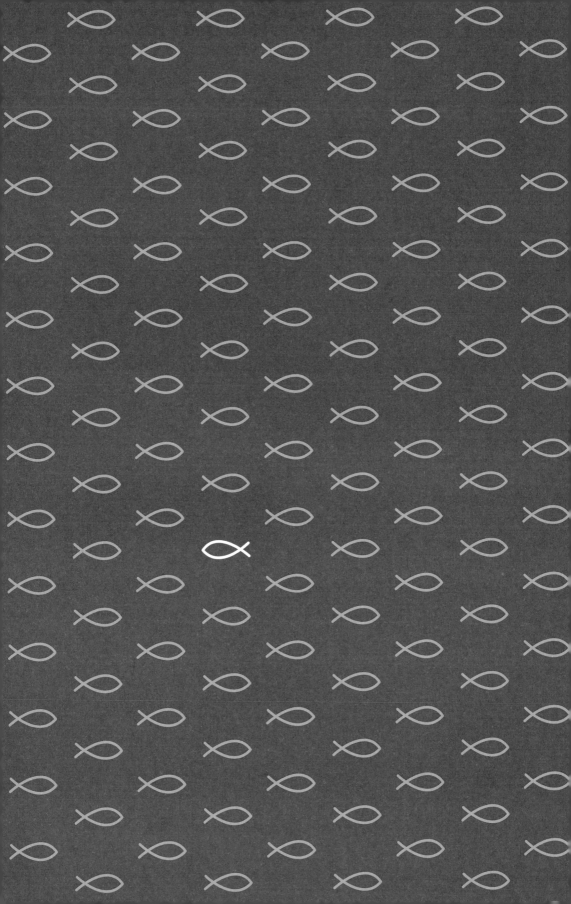

"When you die and go to heaven and you meet God, God is not going to say to you
'Why didn't you become a saint?
Why didn't you discover
the cure for cancer?
Why didn't you change
the world?'
No all God will ask you
at that holy time is
**'Why didn't you
become you?'"**

Elie Wiesel

Be You →

You are unique, a gift. Your life's story so far has shaped you in amazing ways – both the good and bad parts. It's easy to think that being a pioneer is about being like someone else who you look up to and can see is amazing at pioneering. But you are not called to be someone else so don't do comparison. It doesn't matter what anyone else thinks you should be or do either. Your life's work is to be you and become more fully you, to come home to yourself. You have your own blend of frustrations, talents, and passion. Unfurl to heal the world out of those. Like the rest of us you have struggles to deal with and need healing – welcome to the human race. So do some soulwork and learn to look after yourself as well!

Your Purpose
In A Sentence

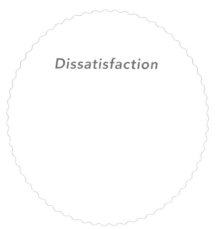

Dissatisfaction

Passion

What is the dissatisfaction that bugs you?

What is the passion you carry?

And what are the talents you have?

Draw three circles on a piece of paper. You can do this on your own but it's also quite good to do with friends, family or your team. In each circle list five to ten things you are dissatisfied with, have a passion for, and have a talent for.

Then distil that list down to one word or phrase for each that is the most important to you. Weave them together into a sentence that says something about you, about who you are and what you are about. This is your purpose.

When I did this with my family we were amazed by it. It really did seem to help get at what we are all about. These are our four to give you some examples:

"I connect with and inspire creative leaders who don't fit in, to help them be true to who they are and to do amazing things."

"I am able to get things done in order to bring liberation where there is oppression."

"Through words, I will help realise the potential in myself and others, to overcome cynicism in the world and self."

"I like creating things that capture niche zeitgeists and do so quietly so that they may resonate louder."

Talents

"I like creating things that capture niche zeitgeists and do so quietly so that they may resonate louder."

You can work on it to get it so it feels like it fits you well. But what you put your energy and effort into will go best if it is aligns with your purpose. There are multiple things you could do that would be a good fit. But it is amazing how many people put their time and energy into things that don't fit them well – either to earn money, or to please someone else, they think it's what they ought to do or they drifted and ended up there.

Mine is the top one so you can see that leading a team that supports pioneers, setting up pioneer training, and putting together this book all fit well. I feel alive when I do them. It fits with my passion. That's what I want to put my energy into. It's my life's work. It's a massive part of who I am and what I am about. It took me a long time to realise that. I did a maths degree because I was good at maths at school and then got a job as a statistician because I thought I'd better use it. But it nearly killed me. I could do it. But I was bored. I certainly wasn't passionate about it. *So I left!*

Ask some friends who know you really well what they think, what they see in you. That can really help if you are stuck.

Do you have any mystical sense of what you are called to? I have sensed things on silent retreats, through prayer, in dreams, and through things others have said - words, phrases, pictures, fragments. They too have helped me sense my purpose and what I believe God has called me to that fits well with who I am. The simplest was sitting in silence on a bench hearing "I have called you to be an advocate for pioneers". I genuinely think that is my life's work now. A photographer took a portrait of me under a stained glass window of Christ's baptism without realising it and that spoke to me profoundly.

The Pioneer Spectrum

Paul Bradbury

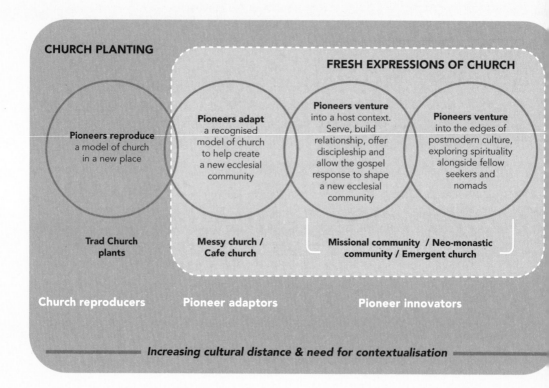

The pioneer spectrum is designed to help you locate yourself and your calling as a pioneer. Not all pioneers are the same. There are common threads in their makeup; creativity, initiating things, building teams and so on. But it's the context that is key.

Pioneers, and pioneering, look different in different contexts. The pioneer spectrum locates different kinds of pioneers on a scale of 'cultural distance.' So, the further to the right you go, the further from the 'home' culture of church you go. And the more of a missional journey into a host culture is needed.

On the left are 'church reproducers' who are really

good at starting churches on the basis of a model that has worked elsewhere. Some creative adaptation may be needed. But essentially these are churches replicated from other churches.

Next on the right are 'pioneer adaptors' who are really good at adapting the way church is often done so that it can engage more effectively with a new context or culture. Often they start with church – but maybe connect with café culture (café church) or all ages (messy church).

Both of these first two kinds tend to start with church in one form or another. That's not the case with the others. With these pioneers theirs is a cross-cultural step, the crossing of a border into someone else's

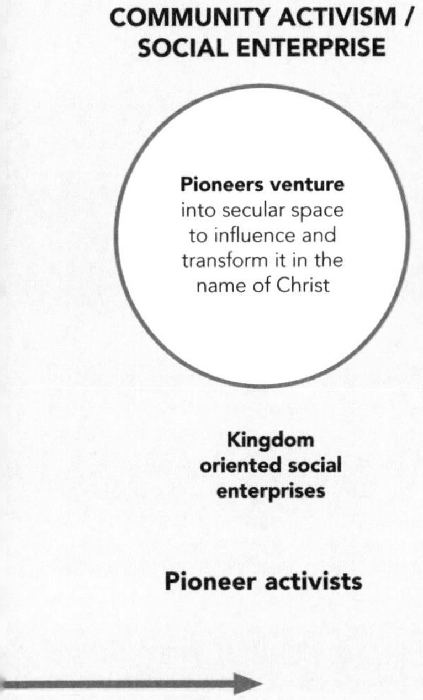

**COMMUNITY ACTIVISM /
SOCIAL ENTERPRISE**

Pioneers venture
into secular space
to influence and
transform it in the
name of Christ

**Kingdom
oriented social
enterprises**

Pioneer activists

world. So here pioneers don't tend to start with church, they start with listening and from listening begin to make connections between the host culture and the gospel. The spectrum describes two kinds of these 'pioneer innovators'. There are those for whom it is a place they working with – for example a new housing estate, an urban centre. Then there are pioneers who work with a particular community or network of spiritual seekers – for example neo-pagans.

With all the four types mentioned so far there is the potential for a new church to arise. Replicators and adaptors start with church anyway, and so church

is planned from the beginning. But with innovators the journey to a new church is more organic, uncertain and less planned. The context needs to help form the new church and this can't be rushed or pre-packaged.

With the final group of pioneers there is little if any intention of starting church. For these 'Pioneer activists' it's the Kingdom of God that is the main thing. These pioneers are driven by the call to help shape the values of the Kingdom in society. A bakery, a coffee roastery, a cleaning company becomes a place that demonstrates what the Kingdom looks like. It might play host to a church, but it might not.

SOULWORK

Being a pioneer is a gift of not fitting in. You see differently. You are acting against the grain so there is bound to be some friction and heat. Because of this, pioneers can get labelled as difficult or awkward. It is important that where we are difficult it is the right kind of difficult. For example, we stand up for those at the edges or we name injustice when we see it. However it can be used as an excuse for not dealing with our own behaviour. There is a wrong kind of difficult which is about selfishness, not dealing with our own stuff, and not taking responsibility. We undermine pioneering when we claim that behaviour is simply part of the gift – it's not. We have simply learned some bad habits. We need to change, grow up, mature, find healing. That requires doing some soulwork.

In organisations, enterprises, charities and the arts there are some things that are appreciated across the board:

Show up on time;
Work hard;
Do what you say you will;
Be completely trustworthy;
Be kind, gentle, good and act from love;
Don't be dominant or forceful;
Listen well to other people.

Habits grow over time both good and bad and you can change them. They are usually deeply ingrained and they are often ways we have learned to cope with the world, to protect ourselves, or to comfort ourselves. Changing them feels scary because we make ourselves vulnerable. But if the heart of pioneering is being you, then it is being and growing into the best version of you so take courage and do some work on your character, habits, behaviour. A good place to start is with some honesty. Get a piece of paper and divide it into two. In one half write down what you are like at your best – how you behave, your habits, your character. In the other half write down what you are like at your worst - your bad habits, addictions, false comforts, ways you behave.

How can you lean into more of the first?
How can you change the second?
What are some old habits you can put off?
What are some new habits you can put on?

We all have different struggles. For some of us **believing** we are **loveable** or have any **worth** is our **battle.**

This is not simple and is a life's work. It is often a case of two steps forward one step back but it is critical work.

Pioneering by its nature meets resistance and invariably goes through the desert on the journey to the new. There are times therefore where you feel anxiety, stress, resistance, fear and anger. That is normal. And it's generally under stress that our worst selves appear. That can be a particularly good time to catch yourself and notice how you behave, to identify what might need some work. Or at least when the stress is over, to take time to reflect back. It's also good to notice yourself when you are in a good place and pay attention to what that place is like so that you can remember and lean into that more when you are not in such a good place.

Practices of self-care and soulwork are so important for this transformative work. The survey shows a wide range of practices that pioneers are engaging in. Prayer is foundational.

We all have different struggles. For some of us believing we are loveable or have any worth is our battle. So this process can be painful because we find it all too easy to focus on our faults which we are already painfully aware of. For others of us we know we are loved but our struggle is we are too sure of ourselves and too pushy so need to let go of control and learn to listen well and give space to others. But whatever our issues are we all need to do some soulwork.

To do this you need a safe space. What is your safe space? That might be with a soul friend, a small group of close friends, a mentor, a counsellor, your team, your partner, a small community who know you well where you are safe to be you, struggles and all.

When pioneering goes wrong it is often this area that derails it – character, behaviour that has gone awry. It might be lack of time or resources, or resistance from the powers that be, but they can often be navigated around. When behaviour derails it is often more messy and harder to pick up the pieces.

This then is the work as much as the work is the work.

What practices do you have of **soulwork** or **self care?**

Retreat

Friendship

Study, reading

Rhythm of prayer, worship, bible reading

Noticing God in wider culture

Running, walking, swimming, football, exercise

Nature, gardening, the outdoors, bee keeping, dog walking

Journalling

Jesus prayer, pray as you go app, morning prayer, Celtic prayer

Varied prayer resources otherwise I get bored and switch off

Spiritual direction, spiritual mentor, soul friend

Taking time out, rest, holiday, day off

Solo time, my hammock

Rhythm of work and rest and keeping boundaries

Being with other pioneers in a safe place where I don't have to explain pioneering

Silence, quiet, meditation, contemplative practices

Mindfulness and well being, checking stress, pacing myself

Hobbies, fun, music, creative stuff, sewing, cooking, comedy nights, gigs, galleries

Gospel singing in the shower

Massage

Constant conversation with God and constant recognition of God's presence

Small group for friendship, support, prayer

Keeping away from the big organisation as much as possible

Counselling, therapy

Sharing food, meals out

Time with partner, family

"To pray is to learn to believe in a transformation of self and world...

which seems
empirically
impossible."

Ched Myers

Flourishing as a PIONEER

ANDY FREEMAN

The World Health Organisation defines Mental Health as "a state of wellbeing in which every individual realises his or her own potential, can cope with the normal stresses of life, can work productively and fruitfully and is able to make a contribution to her or his community." I like this definition because it raises the issue of flourishing - each person being fully themselves at home, at work, in communities. This contrasts with much of the wider conversation around wellbeing which focuses on alleviating problems of stress, anxiety, depression or other mental health concerns.

How can a pioneer flourish?
I'd like to propose four simple ideas.

1. Work out your reserves
It's not always self-evident to think about your mental health when you're fit and healthy. However, it does make perfect sense to consider your reserves of strength and how you can access them when you're well, rather than when you're under pressure or struggling.

What are the things you draw strength from? Work them out when you have time and space so that you know where to go and what to do, when inevitably pressure comes. For example, who are the people you reach out to and find help from? Is everything in place for you to connect with them if times get hard? What are the things that have given you peace and stability in difficult times? Make space for them now, so that when struggles arise you've got a reserve to draw from.

Central to this support will be your spirituality which is like a reservoir you can draw from. Have you spent time working out what reserves of spirituality work well for you and which bolster your wellbeing and personal life? Why not make a wellbeing plan and

include the key elements of your spirituality that are important? Then work hard when you're well to build these as natural life rhythms, so that when life gets tricky you have them there to support you.

2. A being in a place
It's easy for us as pioneers to be overly busy responding to demands that come our way. The place and the task drive us forward, filling our in-trays and making us busy people.

As a pioneer you are still a person, a being not a doing. Don't let the call and vocation of mission define you solely. Put yourself first. This means rest, recuperation and health become valued allies as they keep you going when life gets hard, rather than taking your focus off the 'task.' Learn to be as well as do!

A flourishing pioneer will also allow the place she or he lives and works in to be important. Many people apply the language of Genesis 2, that God "placed Adam in the Garden to emphasise place as a destination God has sent us to. However, Adam (and Eve) also enjoyed the garden, walking with God in the cool of the evening.

I know my wellbeing is added to as I enjoy the garden I'm placed in (Sheffield.) I know that as I reach out to contemporary culture I also gain reserves and resilience from it. Lastly I know that being "placed" here means there are local people whom I need to be wholly myself. This place helps me be me.

3. Psychologically safe
Many pioneers operate within working structures where they are frequently misunderstood. The work of breaking new ground does not always win friends. This dynamic of pioneering can have a mas-

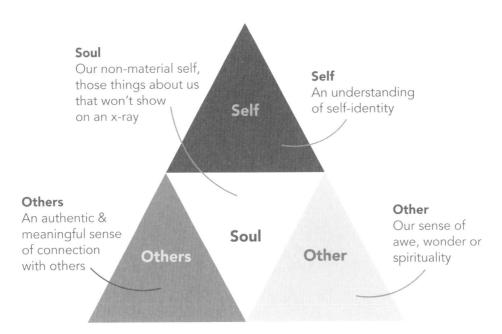

Soul
Our non-material self, those things about us that won't show on an x-ray

Self
An understanding of self-identity

Others
An authentic & meaningful sense of connection with others

Other
Our sense of awe, wonder or spirituality

The Wellbeing Triangle

sive cost. Having the "gift of not fitting in" does not often make us feel safe. If pioneers are truly to thrive, we need environments in which we can ask questions, and where it is ok to challenge and to change things without fear of reprisal.

Amy Edmondson explores how giving employees the psychological safety to be themselves at work and to share opinions freely has led to ground-breaking changes and growth in organisations and charities. She says psychological safety "describes a team climate characterised by interpersonal trust and mutual respect in which people are comfortable being themselves." (The Fearless Organisation). These discoveries have led firms to introduce systems that allow people to know they have the safety to share their ideas without fear of implications or impact on their job prospects.

"My inclination is to ask questions, to get the right people in the conversation and let everyone have a voice. The collective and collaborative process produces a lot of energy – it's the source of creativity and innovation."

4.Self-awareness
Over the last year at Space to Breathe, we have been using a simple framework to help people think about their wellbeing. We call it The Wellbeing Triangle, a geometrically balanced shape that has three equally balanced and important parts. This model balances an awareness of self, authentic connection with others and some sense of what we call "other" - spirituality, wonder, awe or God.

- *What is my sense of self-awareness?*
- *Who do I authentically connect with?*
- *What do I understand to be 'other' and how does it affect me?*

Central to the triangle and to this sense of self-awareness is the soul. We like this word and idea for many reasons. It is both holistic and elusive. It is spiritual in concept but in a way that people understand. It also has a deep heritage.

The Hebrews understood soul as 'Nephesh' which literally translated as "neck." Soul was the connection between the head and the body, the way the whole was brought together.

To thrive as a pioneer, you can plan, be aware of your own spirituality, connect with your environment and work hard to enable your employers to be understanding and permission-giving. But if you don't understand yourself and the way the parts of you connect to make a whole you may struggle. Knowing yourself, knowing who you really are is a natural preliminary step to realising your potential.

"Finding a way in nature is the trellis for where soul searching and sense making happens."

Rewilding The Soul

Johnny Sertin

Some years ago, I came across the concept of rewilding in George Monbiot's Feral. He says that for the world to flourish, a process of rewilding is needed to reverse a commodification of the environment and the domestication of humanity. It got me wondering whether a third element is missing, rewilding the soul.

Spirituality, much like environment and society has been excessively commodified and domesticated often as a result of a colonial straitjacket. It has led to a dogmatic approach to faith ensnared by a regulatory impulse that loses the powerful connection with tradition, the living faith of the dead, becoming imprisoned by traditionalism, the dead faith of the living. Rewilding the soul is about returning to a state of knowing and doing that refounds our story and leads us home to ourselves, to our place in the world and the creative work we are called to.

This subsumption of spirituality can engineer a religious life that feels much like David being asked to wear Saul's armour as we face the giants of today. We struggle about in this inherited suit that in spite of being made for a King, is heavy, cumbersome and not a good fit. But what if we dug deep into our pockets? We might feel the cool assurance of pebbles from the riverbed, the place of our becoming from criss-crossing the rocks and ravines of this life. These small stones of remembrance that are seemingly insignificant compared to the attire of a King, endow us to be who we are formed by the flow of

life and with the agency to face whatever lies before us, adapt, innovate and overcome. Outwardly it was the Philistine who was the giant in the land; inwardly, it was the shepherd boy of the land.

To impact the outer arc of our land today we must explore our inner landscape too and keep those arcs in a constant living conversation. Rewilding the soul is to recognise our need to connect the world within us with the world around us. It's a dance if you like, connecting the inner and outer arcs to be in constant flux and flow as a whole as opposed to separate and objectified. Yes, we need new ideas. But we also need renewed people to create and shape the communities, initiatives and organizations that our world so desperately needs.

Drawing from nature's biorhythms to explore different seasons as stages of development, rewilding the soul could be conceived of as a three-fold process of alchemy – the dark night of the soul; soul searching and creative regeneration. Each phase is part of attending to the shadow work of the soul, the untransformed essence of you that is the gold to come

The dark night of the soul
This first phase recognizes and embraces that our life is not a straight line of events but has moments of doubt, breakdown and being lost. When we see this chaos as part of our becoming it opens up the shadows of our life and leads us into liminal space

where grace begins. Liminality is a season in which chronological time is suspended and we enter a murky twilight context of questions, fears, anxieties and unknowns, Often such space today is swept under the carpet or assuaged by assurances of the light. However good stuff grows in the dark and liminal space is about ritualizing and embracing these times as our friend. Dark work is a "drip and tip" process, not one epiphanic moment but many little "ouches", "oohs", and "ahas" that eventually tip me into a new form. This edge moves me beyond the safety of what I know and into the unknown. The dark forests of liminal space are not meant to be easy to negotiate. Liminality is a lost art as a ritual and getting lost is a critical edge. It seems society would rather live in the "no pain, no gain" mantra. Yet authentic transformation comes from placing my life in a space where I can get lost. It begins the process of drawing out the 'gold' that is hidden there, but needs the breakdown and loss of vision and ethos to emerge.

Soul searching

Growing up between the ages of 1-11 I lived on a 100-acre common on the outskirts of London in an area of natural beauty, part of the Chiltern Hills. We were the last but one tube station on the Bakerloo line. Each day when school was over, I would run off with a couple of friends into the sprawling, wild space of this common. We played sport, organised games, built dens, hunted imaginary foes, climbed trees and ran like feral angels through the bracken.

It was the place where I began intuitively connecting spirituality and nature.

Nature offers a way to explore self-inquiry in the everyday of life. Finding a way in nature is the trellis for where soul searching and sense making happens. She can be our muse showing a way of being in my body, tending to the soil of my heart, ritualising seasons as a litany to remember and return to, enacting daily rhythms and patterns, practicing silence and presence, being in communion with the land and making work that embodies this wholeness. This way in nature frames an inquiry into the landscape of my inner world bringing a dance into play with the living world with all its moods and awareness coursing through it. Is this a time of decay or emergence? What is hibernating right now? What strong winds are blowing through my life?

Creative regeneration

We are all made with an artistry and have this propensity within us. The great Walter Brueggemann says that every totalitarian regime is frightened of the artist simply because they seek to keep alive the imagination as their principal agency, to keep on 'conjuring and proposing futures alternative to the dominant norm.' Signs of rewilding the soul are when we value and enact the imagination before implementation believing the 'absurdity of hope' to be stronger than society's take of reality.

I find I hesitantly consider myself artistic,

We are all made with an artistry and *have this propensity within us.*

a self-styled space maker for soul. I am learning to be at home as an artist. albeit I wear it somewhat awkwardly. Having courage to stand in our creativity is critical, bringing fuller, more-than-intellectual ways of knowing into the outer arc of our work that in turn reshapes the fundamental ways mission and spirituality is structured. It supports there is a knowledge landscape broader than empirical knowing and offers artful practice as a way of reuniting spirituality with mission, into the same dance between the inner and outer arcs.

Bio spirituality – a universal ground for pioneers
Rewilding the soul is a type of spirituality essential not only to survive, but also to thrive in the 21st century. My evangelical roots were a good place to conceive the prophet Micah's injunction 'to act justly and love mercy.' But to perpetuate this outer arc of good I also need to tap into the root from which this source comes. Rewilding teaches us a way of knowing and doing that creates a way of being that becomes a feedback loop for remaining centred in this truth.

I describe this as a bio-spirituality for three reasons. First, it reconciles my story with the story of the "big book" of nature, experiencing the world as lover, an essential and life-giving partner who I engage with as a co-creator, collaborator. Second, it frames time through the seasons to form liminal and regenerative space that inhabits a place for transformation. Finally, it affirms artistic agency and the embrace of the sensuous self as a performative, reflexive, perceptive, intentional, indeterminate, emergent, embodied being-in-the-world.

At a leadership workshop I attended a few years ago, "go big or go home!" was a phrase I heard many times. The premise was to invoke us to do extraordinary work in the world. However, what if what good really looks like and the world needs, is to "go home"?! To rediscover the concept of home in me, my family, community, profession and planet? To embark on a search in the cracks and crevices of everyday, to find a place that invokes a sense of belonging and meaning where I am formed? Where the work that defines me comes to light beyond the bright lights of political governance, religious bodies or corporate culture trapped in a closed system?

Rewilding the soul begins as a first-person quest. It leads us on the road back home to ourselves. It is a journey that coexists between displacement and homecoming. Without the pain of displacement, we have no awareness of our desire for home. Yet without the discovery of home we have no compass to guide us as we explore the road ahead. This seems much more important than the arrogance of "going big'. Life is more complex and shaped in the everyday. So perhaps small fits where big doesn't. We are pioneers who make "islands of sanity" - small places where we can incubate "home" in a web of relationships nurtured by a culture of participation emancipated from metrics that demand bigger is always better. Here, there is a seedbed for the imagination, emergent enterprise and regenerative practice. Such a way might tip us in us into another world on the horizon.

"Home is where the heart is.
It stands for the sure centre
where individual life is shaped
and from where it journeys
forth... In a sense that is
exactly what spirituality is:
the art of homecoming."

John O'Donohue

Spiritua

Michael Mitton is a spiritual director, writer and trainer. He has been a good and wise friend and guide to many pioneers.

Can you describe the kind of thing you might do in spiritual direction?

The primary focus of the conversation is to help the person track their own particular journey with God. So I have a range of clients and I find some come highly prepared - they have issues that are developing in their lives that they wish to talk to me about and so the material in the session is fairly closely connected with what they have prepared. And there will be others that come not really sure what they might talk about and they will find that just by starting to have conversation things will surface that are important to attend to.

How might it develop over time?

The real quality that develops is trust. Initially of course people will inevitably be feeling their way. They'll be asking whether they can trust me: can they trust me to be confidential? Can they trust me not to judge them? That would be an extremely important quality because they might want to share things about which they feel ashamed. Can they trust me not to be directive by which I mean over-directive pushing them into lifestyle or even values that is not theirs? So there's a whole collection of trusts that can only be developed over time.

How did you get into it?

Firstly by receiving spiritual direction myself. I have had the same spiritual director for forty years now so I saw the benefit in having a trusted friend with whom I could disclose material that I probably wouldn't disclose to the rest of the world. I then found myself warming to the power of listening and that was particularly evident in my work with the Acorn Christian Healing Foundation. I found that listening was one of the most powerful pastoral tools I'd come across and certainly empowering for the person being listened to. I felt I'd learned so much about listening and I wanted to offer that to others.

You seem to like pioneers. How come?

I have to confess that my experience of much of regular church life is that it does not inspire me. I have been a church minister. I've been committed to it. I love the Church of England; I've worked for it, with it, been at the heart of it and at the edge of it. But what lit me up most has been meeting people who are pioneers who are developing visions of church that are a great deal more inspiring than the more regular ones.

Is accompaniment the same for pioneers or does it help to have an awareness of the challenges they face?

My experience working directly with a group of pioneers in Derby diocese which I did for a number

Direction

of years was that they required a particular kind of listening. I felt what they needed was somebody who got them. They felt that many of their colleagues who were in more regular kinds of work didn't really get the kind of work they were trying to do. The charism I prayed for very much was a profound understanding of what it was they were trying to achieve through their ministry and to pray that I could somehow see the world through their very creative eyes. Going back to trust again, the pioneers I work with now in spiritual direction need to trust me that they can talk about a world in which they feel quite vulnerable because their ministry is different to other colleagues. They can talk about it and I can hold it and not regard them as weird, loopy, unfaithful to the church or whatever.

One of our learnings over the years has been that pioneering goes best when it comes from who you are not from some imagined other way you think you ought to be. In your book Dreaming of Home you suggest that 'coming home to yourself' is a hugely important. Why is that so significant?
A pioneer has to be quite self-assured. They meet many unusual challenges and some of the challenges are to their identity. So they do need to do some work on 'who is it that God has made me?', to be settled in that. Oddly enough one of the pressures can come from the pioneering world itself because some pioneers are actually people who are not

weird, wild, radical, always thinking in very different ways, but they are just quite humble people who have caught a vision for how to do church differently. Once they start comparing themselves with people they might regard as high flyers in the pioneering world they can feel quite easily condemned in a way – they're not doing the great and mighty things they see others doing. For people like that it's really important to say God has made you who you are and be settled in that. There's pressure from the church which can label pioneers in all kinds of ways. So you have to be sure of your own identity. Maybe the most important one is for missional reasons because I would hope that one of the high values of a pioneering community is that it is a place where anybody can come and they can be themselves. That's not going to happen if the pioneer is not behaving in such a way as suggests they are comfortable with who they are.

Soulwork is how we've come to describe that process of sorting through your own stuff. How do you see that process for pioneers?
It's really important. For example I can think of a pioneer who had to put a huge amount of effort into persuading their Bishop that what they were doing was worthwhile. You gain a lot of inner strength from affirmation from whoever is your boss. And if you are in a relationship with your boss

▶

where they are constantly questioning whether you are doing a worthwhile job or not, that takes you quite deep into yourself. You have to find a security in God where you feel very sure of your calling. Quite a lot of us go through wobbly moments with our calling. We'll be working away and think 'did I get this completely wrong? Would it have been so much easier if I had done a regular church job?' So from time to time pioneers can be taken into places of quite painful insecurity where securities that can be granted in the regular stream of things they are deprived of to some extent. And there can be a more raw dependance on God. Then as well as identity and calling, the other thing I see in many pioneers is that the shape of their faith can move. Some feel they can become a good deal more liberal. For those who've started from an evangelical starting point that can be disturbing.

We have observed this with students and come to describe it as a sort of theological homelessness. It's probably because they are in contexts where the answers you had don't make sense any more and you are looking for new language.
For many Christians their spirituality is defined in the context of the Christian community where there is a lot of common ground. The pioneer's spirituality is being defined by the missional edge and therefore different questions are being asked of them. So there has to be a revisiting of old assumptions. For some there is actually a faith crisis that has to happen and an old faith that does have to be dismantled and a new one found.

Is that why the desert experience is inevitable on the journey to the new?
Many do feel a desert place and we shouldn't be afraid of it. It is a place of deep creativity. But as Jesus found in his desert journey it got him into some very hard questions, very personal questions. Issues of power have to be faced in the desert. These can be uncomfortable things for which people do need a soul friend or guide where they can talk honestly about what is happening for them in that place and feel it is safe to do so.

Are there practices that can help?
Three spring to mind. One is some kind of rhythm of retreat - an annual retreat is really important. I'd also go for a monthly quiet day. Pioneers can get very busy and I would encourage each one to have at least a day a month when they are stepping back from the work and it's just a day for them to review how they are with God and to renew that relationship. The other thing is some kind of cell group. It's important for them to meet with others. When I was in Derby we formed the company of pioneers that quickly became a safe place where pioneers could meet and be very honest with each other and I was really impressed how honest they became. It was a confidential support group and there was no having to explain themselves. There was a high degree of empathy in the group. It can be quite a lonely thing which is why I think a group is important. Oh and spiritual direction!

How do people go about finding a spiritual director?
Pioneers can find it difficult to find someone. A good spiritual director will adapt and become familiar with the world that the pioneer is trying to talk about. Some pioneers in seeking a spiritual director may find someone who just doesn't get their world and they will need to find somebody else. It may be that some pioneers need to train as spiritual directors so they can help one another.

"A pioneer is someone who sees future possibilities and works to bring them to reality"

Beth Keith

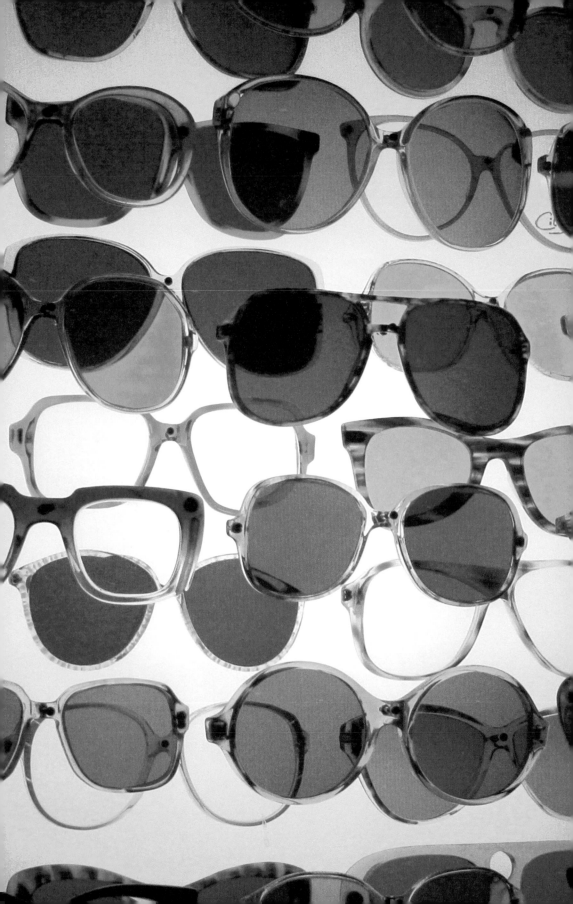

See →

Pioneering is a gift of sight. If business as usual is straight ahead, you look sideways or behind and notice things that most people miss. Because you can see it, it is obvious but after a while you begin to realise that what seems obvious to you is far from it for others, especially if they are quite happy with the status quo. They may well be blind to what you see. There are huge parallels with artists who make art out of looking in fresh ways, and with prophets who are called seers in some traditions. Their currency too is imagination. Imagination is hugely under-rated. Anything that has been made was first imagined. Without imagination we are simply stuck and going nowhere!

How have you learned to see or imagine
differently?

Through being around other creative people

Watching how others innovate

Stepped away from that which I knew... the old way

Living in the world and not the church

Hanging out with young people

Loving art

Design thinking

Question everything

Suffering and failure is part of
the process of paying attention

Paying attention to self, others, place
and God finds the connections

Double listening – to context and to the Holy Spirit

Prayer, scriptures, contemplative practices

Being exposed to new people, theological ideas, difference

Through some Holy Spirit inspiration

From the margins

Experiencing other cultures

Noticing the people who are not reached
and finding new ways of connection

Spending time with local people
and seeing life through their lens

See what's going on around my local
community and see what God is up to

Through years of being part of
things that encouraged difference

Having the courage to try things
and not worry if they failed

Risk. There is always a new, scary and risky horizon into the
unknown that the Spirit will lead you towards if you listen.

Going with the flow, letting go control

I haven't – it's how I see things. Other people
don't see what I see, and yet to me it's obvious

Pioneers see things at the edge,

things that other people

don't notice.

They are often surprised to find

other people haven't noticed

what they see because

it seems **so obvious!...**

but only once you have seen it.

FOR A START

It's sometimes a challenge knowing where to start, where to dive in. These three questions are good for a start.

What is bugging you?
Dissatisfaction, restlessness or even downright anger are good places to look, to notice, to pay attention. Our passion is often about overcoming something we have noticed that bugs us.

For me I get so frustrated with the disconnect between the way church is done and the people I know outside it. It feels like they are on other planets to each other. It is that gap that drives me to want to imagine it can be done differently in a way that makes sense and connects with those outside. What are you frustrated with? What are you dissatisfied with? What can you see that is broken? What is the gap between reality and what you hope for? What or who is being overlooked? What are you angry about? What is bugging you?

We can notice lots of things like that. But is there something you come back to again and again like a splinter that you can't seem to get rid of. Not a surface thing or a selfish thing but a deep thing. You keep seeing it. It's likely it cropped up in your purpose statement. That's a big clue that you should give that some more attention. Look at it, notice it, see it, pray about it, reflect on it, chew over it.

What are you longing for?
Another way of coming at this is to notice your deep desires, your longings. They too will give you a clue as to where to pay some more attention. I am not talking about selfish desires or appetite that can easily be distractions or distortions but a deep yearning, an ache. Name it, see it, allow it to materialise.

What is possible?
Then a third question to ask is what you can imagine that can be done about your frustration, and about your longing. What is possible? There are likely many things. But is there a particular thing you can do with the resources and skills you have? Is there an idea? An inkling? A hunch you have?

We tend to think that seeing relates to the third question only – the imagining part. But actually frustration and longing are a critical part of seeing too.

Pioneers see things at the edge, things that other people don't notice. They are often surprised to find other people haven't noticed what they see because it seems so obvious! It is of course, but only once you have seen it.

ideas

Creativity is like a muscle. There are definitely things you can do to exercise. If you use it, it grows stronger. Pioneers are usually good at this but here are a few things we've learned on the way.

Get away from your desk
Where do you come up with ideas? Probably not by sitting down and thinking I must come up with an idea! So get out. Walk, play, exercise, go and look at art, relax. When you do come up with an idea have a place you make a note of it.

Bounce ideas around with others
Invite some people who will be passionate about your longing and who are sparky to meet for a beer or coffee or meal i.e. somewhere informal. And bounce ideas round with them. Have some paper, pens, post its and so on to capture the conversation.

Hang out with creative people
Creativity is simply in the air around some people. Hang out with them, enjoy their curiosity and playfulness. It will rub off on you.

Get beyond your first idea
The more ideas you have the better off you are. So once someone has come up with an idea, don't let anyone get defensive about it. Either build on it or come up with more ideas.

Break the rules

In most areas of life there are habits and patterns. We think down familiar routes and tracks. Creative thinking requires getting knocked off course and breaking the usual pattern, the usual ways of doing things, the norms. In whatever area you are thinking about slay a few sacred cows. Name the rules and deliberately break them. See where it leads you. This can be a hard one for church people as churches have become cultures that are very defended around doing things the right way, or having the right beliefs. But those rules too need breaking to find new paths.

Mess around
Play with crazy ideas. Mess around. Laugh a lot!

Get outside your area
The brain is great at taking something in one area and making a connection with it in another. So it really pays to get outside your area of familiarity and see what you find. Make connections back. In particular look at art, photography, film, design – other creative work. And visit other cultures – cross a border and look back.

Fail
Failure comes from taking risks, trying things so don't be afraid to fail. It's the flipside of creativity.

Ask questions
What if? Why not? are two pretty good ones for pioneers. Be curious. Don't accept the right answer. Question everything.

Get provoked
A lot of ideas are a result of being provoked. Coronavirus is a good example. Churches couldn't meet in buildings so that provoked them to come up with all sorts of ways of being a community of disciples that they would not have done otherwise.

on

"Art is pushing at the boundaries we thought were fixed. The convenient lies fall; the only boundaries are the boundaries of our imagination. How much can we imagine? The artist is an imaginer."

Jeanette Wintersen in Art Objects

"When you start out in art you have no idea what you are doing. This is great. People who know what they are doing know the rules, and know what is possible and impossible. You do not. And you should not. If you don't know it's impossible it's easier to do. And because nobody's done it before, they haven't made up rules to stop anyone doing that again, yet."

Neil Gaiman in Art Matters

"**Risk** – the enemy of your own and other peoples certainty. A state of **optimistic dissatisfaction**, of relentless **questioning**..

art

"Reshape the world to contain the artwork you make, to create a new reality – because it's never been enough just to make the art"

Creative Stance

"Passion is the spur that makes us want to know more. It provides the impulse for the thoughtful enquiry that generates the knowledge which fires our imagination to come up with ideas. These lead to the experiments that eventually result in the production of a realised concept. That is the path that creativity takes.

Will Gompertz in Think Like An Artist

A preoccupation with **quality** without regard for the **established order.**" Creative Stance

GARFIELD

IKEA

IKEA

HB

WINNER 1210 HB

WRITE STYLE HB

hi precision WRITING

KPMG Peat Marwick McLintock

GERMANY

Ref.0977   Kajal Black

Seeing what God is doing...

Sue Steer was appointed by Churches Together in Leicestershire as Pioneer Community Worker for New Lubbesthorpe, a new housing area outside of Leicester. She was appointed before any houses were built so began with a blank slate and a blank piece of land to pioneer something new and build community.

How do you see what God is doing?

The story that led to me working in Lubbesthorpe began in March 2011 when Churches Together noticed a plan submitted to Blaby District Council to build 4,250 homes. They wrote to Blaby District Council expressing an interest in 'Building Community in Lubbesthorpe'. A quick response was received and a group was formed which was warmly received by the Council. During the next few years Churches Together worked with the council and the surrounding villages towards a vision for Lubbesthorpe and in 2014 began to look at providing a 'Community Development Worker'. I was appointed in 2016. But I think that seeing had begun five years earlier through looking prayerfully outwards.

How about when you first started?

It was such a blank canvas. There was nothing there, no people doing stuff. So the place I looked was to the founding story of the place and wondered what God had been doing before anyone had got involved. I found out that the family who were the landowners talked about Lubbesthorpe as a place where people would live and work and play. That fascinated me as they had a vision of community. God seemed to be at work there before anyone arrived and we were joining in with that. God can be at work in people who aren't Christians. Another thing that helped early on was the story of Abraham going with his tent. I think the story came to me because off the connection with going to a new land. But it has carried through - for example the hub moves and it still feels like it's a tent! It literally gets picked up and put in a new area.

What else helps you discern?

I do a lot of talking to people and asking what they feel and what they want to see. That is in conversations and sometimes in more formal ways. For example, we did a listening week to get people to talk about what they thought was good and what they wanted to see happen in the future. We took the lead but the district council, land trust and developer joined in. We had stuff round the wall for people to put ideas on and say what they thought was good and so on. When you start as a lone pioneer you have to work with the assets of others. It grows so fast so there's no way you can do everything. And you need to embrace the other stakeholders that come in and not be afraid. The school says 'we want to have a community space' so it makes sense to work with that rather than be protective.

...and joining in

I also trust my gut instinct which I take to be about listening to the Spirit. It's a difficult call, isn't it? Are you just seeing what's happening naturally or is that where God is at work or both? One puzzle was the tension between building community and the expectation of growing Christian community. I found that the Fresh Expressions stages of listening, loving, serving, building community were natural. But it doesn't mean people want to move to the next stage - explore discipleship! The lightbulb moment for me was seeing community development stuff elsewhere, doing a module with CMS on community development and talking with Anna Ruddick. I saw small groups of Christians making a massive impact on their community and that's good enough. That helped me see that I needed to hold both authentically and let the community stuff which was happening be a good in its own right rather than foisting another agenda onto it and trust the process and trust God.

Are there other moments that happened where you sensed God at work in a particular way?
The funding model from Churches Together was for three years and then reducing year on year with the hope that something sustainable could grow. We went to see the developer to talk about this and asked if he would contribute. He said how much he loathed the way the housing industry had gone and that he wanted to see change. There was lots of talk about place-making in the industry but invariably they simply made money and moved on. I felt God was working through him. By us going cap in hand to him it had started him thinking how he could impact the whole housing industry. He offered us an amount for each house sold paid into our charity and then asked what we would do with it. That pushed us to think beyond what we would normally do. It's potentially a substantial amount of money and could sustain things over a 20-year period.

That's so great! I wonder if that might become a model elsewhere? Who is involved with you now?
Groups of volunteers are involved in different things. I am often talking to them about how their things are going and then it might change. But we are now shifting structure to set up a CIC (community interest company) and there are three of us who will be directors. The others are residents. Discernment also sometimes involves difficulty so getting that group right had its challenges. I quickly learned that you have to find people who share the vision and values. Then at the core we have a group of about ten who are part of Tuesday night missional community which meets every other week. That group have just started a monthly cycle of things on a Sunday afternoon - a community meal and table talk, a walk, mossy church (a cross between forest church and messy church)

▶

and community action of some sort. But because of Coronavirus we haven't completed one month yet! We talked about it just being having a go so it can change as we feel our way.

Hearing your story you seem to be in a landscape and situation that is constantly changing so you have to be flexible, adaptive, light touch, and being able to pivot is essential. I think innovation is like that - you feel your way, try stuff out, learn from it, go again and try and make sense of it all the time being prayerful and attentive.
Absolutely. It's quite tiring! I know I am a firestarter more than a maintainer which has worked well because the community end up taking things on.

Have you got ways you look back in terms of seeing?
Every year with the management group we have a strategy day. It's about reflecting on what we have done and what we are going to do. I am now rebuilding the management committee because the original people have moved on and the structure is changing. The Christian community and the CIC is taking a lot of time and energy at the moment but is important foundations. At the stage we are at now we have been looking back at our story so far and are asking again what has God been doing through that?

Is there anything else by way of practices that helps you see that you haven't mentioned yet?
Going away from the community to take time out on retreat. I journal and I have a spiritual accompanier. To be honest that is what has kept me going. It can be quite hard going at times, trying to work things out and adapting to the change that happens around you. I think that's part of the seeing though, needing to sit in the messiness until the way becomes clear. Retreating is important to me too, I neglected last year and I really regret that. Just taking those days out to go through journals, reflect back, find the themes, and learn some lessons is critical. Then sometimes I find an idea from a book that really seems right for the moment. A recent example is that I read a book by Dave Andrews about the word ekklesia in the bible, which gets translated as 'church'. He was saying that it was a political and not a religious term for a community council. So rather than Christians being set apart it is about being set as a part of the community. So I have come to see the CIC is more like that idea of church than those who imagine it as meeting every week on a Sunday!

New Lubbesthorpe timeline

2011
Planning Application to build 4250 homes in Lubbesthorpe. Churches Together (CTog) approach Council to offer help in building a healthy community.

2012/13
Planning Permission granted. Vision shared with local residents and CTog by the Council. Ecumenical prayer group and action group formed and CTog outline to the council how they might help in community building.

2014
CTog agree to fund a Community Development Worker. The Council ensure the Developer will provide the community worker with temporary premises to work out of by the time 50 houses were built.

2016
Sue Steer is employed as Pioneer Community Worker and starts in September as the first house foundations were laid. Time spent getting to know the surrounding suburbs, community groups and main stakeholders including the overall Site Developer and housebuilders. Hangs around in the sales offices and meets people before they move in.

I do a lot of talking to people and asking what they *feel* and what they want to **see.**

2017
First residents move in, all are visited with a Welcome Pack.
Seasonal outdoor events are created as a way of helping people meet their new neighbours.

2018
The temporary accommodation arrives in the form of a large, well furnished portacabin known as The Hub. Sue encourages residents to start community interest groups and residents ask for a Baby and Toddler Group to be created. Brewed Awakening coffee morning, a walking group, couch to 5K and book club emerge. A group of three of us meet on a Tuesday to pray and eat together which grows to about ten and is named Heart & Soul.

2019
350 houses occupied. Welcome visits continue with a team of residents. Seasonal events grow rapidly with around 700 at Christmas light switch on. Mossy Church starts and around eight families come along.
Listening week with residents and stakeholders.
In September The Hub moves to a new location and is out of action for four months. Temporarily located in the newly built school. Some groups stop, some move into homes, some remain outside.
Start the process to create a CIC with indigenous community leaders to move to a long term sustainable Community Development organisation. Good relationships built with the Developer means financial help is offered to continue the Community Development work.
Agree to work in Partnership with the Land Trust who will care for the open space.

2020
The Hub re-opens on the edge of what will be the new Village Square. We start to re-imagine the future in our new location. Continued partnership with the school means our young families activities continue in the school, we start planning to use the school allotment for Mossy Church.
Heart & Soul start a Sunday afternoon gathering.
Covid-19 arrives and the community look to us to lead the community response for those needing help. We start re-imagining community engagement once again.

"I'm not just CRAZY-

I'm gifted in seeing things differently!"

We are all wearing glasses

None of us has the truth. We all have a take. We see from a particular viewpoint. That doesn't mean there isn't truth – of course there is. It's just a bit harder to get at. Our view has been shaped by our upbringing, culture, parents, education, class, ethnicity, ways we have been wounded and how we responded to those experiences and so on. That worldview isn't simply a doctrinal thing, a set of beliefs. It's much more deeply rooted and shapes us more than we know. Beneath the surface of our lives are hidden persuaders. The scary thing is most of us just assume our take is normal, the way things are. But actually we are all wearing glasses. We all see through lenses.

If we don't realise we have a particular way of seeing we're in danger of imposing our way of seeing and doing things onto others, to universalise it and ignore or marginalise other ways of seeing.

It's really hard to just step back and take off your glasses and say 'here is my worldview' because it is so deeply embedded. But it is critical to at least be aware you have a set of glasses and to grow in awareness of the contours of that.

One of the best ways to notice you have a set of glasses is to cross a border, go to another culture and discover people who see and do things differently. What you thought was normal turns out to be local. We are much more likely to get a richer picture if we get round the table in conversation with a range of perspectives.

There is usually a dominant way of seeing. That seeing is about how we do things round here, what we think and how we behave, what we value, what is sacred and what is profane, the way things are. For example in churches this relates to theology, belief, the way we do church. By virtue of being a pioneer you see differently. It's obvious to you that the dominant way of seeing is simply a take and that other ways of seeing are essential. Perhaps the dominant way of seeing worked once but no longer makes sense in today's world. Or perhaps it is shaped in a way that just doesn't make sense to those on the outside of church cultures. But when you point this out it can be received as a threat, heretical even. So you are constantly perceived as making trouble but actually you just see something differently and want to imagine new possibilities!

We are also prone to dominating too. It's seductive to believe that our way of seeing is better than others. So it is crucial as pioneers that we learn to hold ourselves lightly, have humility about our own take on things and be prepared to let it go. This is particularly the case in mission when we cross a border and dwell with those in other cultures and at the fringes. We have something to share, the story of Christ, ideas and possibilities of change and a better world. But the challenge is not to impose those from the outside but to let go of our ways of doing things and offer anything as a gift in humility. Some of our things may be really unhelpful after all. It's a normal experience for pioneers to experience a sense of theological homelessness. The ways you

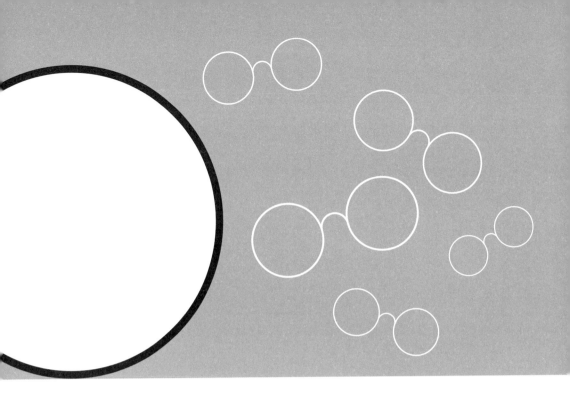

had framed theology don't make sense in the new environment so you are searching for new language that makes the world differently. Then new ways of seeing and doing things can emerge and grow from the inside of those spaces – local or contextual theology, new forms of church, new ways of doing things, new social enterprises, new community projects. They will of course go best when they are led by people who are local so something else to see over time is who the local leaders might be.

How do you do that really well? If you are on the right half of the pioneer spectrum (p64) it is really quite a tricky set of skills. If you are on the left hand end replicating or adapting a model, it is a lot simpler though there are probably bigger risks of dominating. This question is essentially about cross-cultural mission. Fortunately, people have been thinking about this question for hundreds of years and participating in mission both badly and well and we can learn from both.

The heart of mission is Jesus Christ the pioneer of our faith. So we come back again and again to the stories of Jesus and his mission, soaking ourselves in those as we seek to see and follow in his way. We also seek the life and animation of the Spirit who is dynamically alive in and with us beckoning us into the future.

Mission is a lens for pioneers. It's a really helpful way to look at the story of Christ, at theology, at church, at the world. In some parts of the church and world mission is a dirty word because it has been associated with Western domination and colonisation. And indeed it can still be used that way so we tread cautiously. But we think it's possible with awareness for it to be a really good set of glasses that brings good news, healing, transformation and resists the powers.

There's no neutrality. Everyone has a take. Some people opt to sit on the sidelines rather than participate and risk getting things wrong but that too is a take. But pioneers are not really sideline kind of people! Take courage and get into the arena (as Brene Brown puts it), step out but do so with love, grace, humility, kindness and with a hefty dose of self-awareness not taking yourself too seriously.

We have pondered what the aspects of that lens are for pioneers at CMS and have distilled it down. We call it True North, where True North is a metaphor for the pull or orientation of everything towards joining in God's mission of the healing of all things. It's not perfect but captures something of the charism or gift that pioneers bring and the way you see the world. That is included towards the end of this book.

Build →

New things start in all sorts of ways. Some are meticulously planned. Some take a model of what has worked in one place and reproduce it. Some just seem to emerge. In some cases, people try and start one thing and something else gets catalysed. But if stuff is going to happen ideas and dreams have to be given legs. There is work to be done. At times pioneering is really exciting but it is also work, daily grind, chipping away, determination, dealing with unexpected roadblocks to realise and build the vision.

A Time To

Gavin Mart is a pioneer in North Wales who has pioneered in the arts, through housing, in social enterprise and building communities of disciples in and around those things.

Shannon Hopkins ran a fashion business, church planted, developed a network for young leaders, traveled to London as a missionary from Texas and developed Matryoshka Haus as an umbrella for launching social enterprises that do good in the world.

Ben Thorpe is an ordained pioneer minister in the Church of England and he is in Newton Leys, Milton Keynes where he is building community and a church family St Joseph's starting from nothing three years ago. We had a conversation about how pioneers build things out of what they see.

G: I think of pioneering as a farm. The products of the field are the fruit of the pioneering work. A farm needs a cycle. There are periods when the farm is in natural harvest and good things just happen when it's fertile and the work is the gathering in, the harvest and then the storage. There is a time to plough, to plant, to harvest and let the land recover. For me whenever a project has some traction that is the time of harvest. You're the farmer, the builder, tinkering, fertilising, planting the seed and so on. You gather, store, distribute it. There can be a season where the ground won't yield any more. Those times are liminal - unknown - and the pioneer needs to be able to hold the ground in those times and be faithful trusting that the land will recover. The Giver Of Life will do the restorative work.

J: How does that relate to the pioneering you have done?

G: I am 25 years in and there' been a turnover of about four periods of seven years where there's been those kind of cycles. It's only now looking back I can recognise that. In the rough and tumble you don't think so much. Looking at the cycle is helpful for me because otherwise it can feel like chaos.

S: I have been in the UK for 16 years. I think Matryoshka Haus has had two cycles - one of radical experimentation when we launched 13 projects. The second half was about mining that to train and equip others. Then that has just come to an end and new things are starting.

J: What's it like at the start of the build process when you have a blank sheet?

B: The emptiness we started with freaked the hell out of me because there was that blank sheet. I was told to do nothing for six months apart from looking and meeting people and trying to see what God was doing. That was our instinct to see what was already going on and join in rather than impose a new structure. It took me to the brink mentally doing nothing in that way. I had to trust that God was at work, would provide people, seeds would germinate. Lo and behold three and half years later and amazingly we do have a community. But the start is hard.

Build

J: Shannon you have built a number of projects and supported others doing that. What have you learned about that process?

S: I love the introduction to this section where you say sometimes things start through a plan and sometimes they emerge. Even when I have a plan it's important I let things emerge. I would say the first thing is getting really clear on your idea. Then what is the smallest version of that you can experiment with so you can get some quick wins and learn on the way. And it's crucial you know what end you are aiming for. It's always been important that you find the people you want to build with. For me when I came to London the initial building was by starting to experiment with others and to see what was taking root. It takes quite a while to build something which you can see in the timelines of the stories in this book. But often you can do good work on the way. A recent thing for us has been getting people to connect to their founding story. Pioneering goes well when as Buechner says you connect your deepest gladness with the world's greatest need. I guess it's another way of saying be you!

B: I agree on getting clear on the vision. Our vision was to be an extended family. We were sure that we were meant to do that so we said no to other things and stuck to what we felt called to. You have to be fairly focused.

G: I have found that when i have lost track the money hasn't been there. When I am in line with the vision and what God is calling us to we have actually never been without. The storehouse has never been empty. God works through our dreams and visions. You have been called. I am with you, I go ahead of you to make the road straight, and you need to stay on that track. There will be a fallow time at some point. God is guiding you. It's obvious when you fall off that track. When you recognise it, you come back to God and the vision and say I am lost and get a sense of what you should do and resources are released and there is plenty.

J: One of the questions I asked in the research was about tools that have been helpful. Most of the answers were things like spiritual practices but I was expecting practical tools. What tools do you think are the most helpful?

S: My first career was in fashion so I did sales, marketing, strategy. That learning has helped me a lot in the church space. They are transferable skills. You have to have a sense of what stacks up. For example I experienced when people are over leveraged and the cash flow doesn't work. I learned so much from that. If you don't have the maths you need someone who does!

G: This is my working accounts for a project. (At this point Gav shows us a spreadsheet for one of his projects!) You work on a cash flow, forecast, some predictions. You have to run a profit and loss and a cash flow. You keep track of where you are at and

what's happening on the farm! You are lost if you don't know where you are at especially when you employ staff. It's tricky because many of the things we value like building community, goodwill, people taking steps on faith don't show on the spreadsheet. The pioneer has to balance those with the number crunching. And is what you are building contributing into the kingdom? Is your vision and ethos clear and written into the hard coding of your project? The tools need to serve the vision. It can be easily flipped when you lose sight of the vision. It's a trap we all fall into. I did some of this stuff at college but you learn it by doing it really.

S: You can lose track because we don't measure. That's why measuring impact is important.

B: We found Mike Breen's Growing Discipleship Culture helpful - is that a tool? He says to look out for people of peace so we said let's go and make friends and it grew from there. There are 10000 people on the local Facebook page. We noticed that every time there's a meal Jesus is at someone else's house so we are going to do whatever other people are doing. So curry club - yes I'll join that. Football - I'll do that. Is there anyone wanting to do gardening or go for a bike ride? The WI, being at the school gates? It's all that kind of stuff really. After six months we stuck our head above the parapet and one Sunday a month we would meet at my house and do something - we did something different every week and tried to leave it as open as we could to connect with people we were meeting. We began to meet weekly on a Tuesday evening for prayer. And we slowly built up from that. It shifted to two Sundays a month and developed a rhythm

of life. We have now grown and meet in the primary school doing a cafe church type thing. When we meet we eat so we always do a shared lunch. We are always mindful of different levels so try and make it open and welcoming for all. Three and a half years on we have about 70 people who would self identify as being part of St Joseph's. To some people it would just look like church. But to church types it doesn't! It's church for people who don't do church - over half are unchurched or dechurched. We have a lot of women who had grown up in faith, got married to someone who wasn't and drifted out of it. But somehow through what we are doing have had it rekindled and are excited about it again. So I have so many men who are unchurched but happy to associate with us and engage at various levels. We also do pods which is groups of three to five deliberately low key so it's easy for people without faith.

J: How do you factor in the money when you build something? One of the survey questions is freedom or money and the vast majority identify freedom as what they value. But equally you have to find a way to make money work.

B: I am very fortunate in that this role came with five years funding then being tapered for another five. That's unusual! But we're three and a half years in so we are only a year and a bit away from when the money starts reducing. So we have been having this conversation. Our whole church could exist for £5000 a year because it's just based on being a community. The big cost is me! One option is I go part time and develop another flow and we continue from the giving we have. Or as a church do we start an enterprise?

G: I felt uncomfortable with the old giving process in communities. Somebody always holds the purse strings above you. I felt very called to try and step into the gap that i felt the church had omitted from its structures. In a lot of ways the set up of the established churches - the model doesn't work. It relies on people filling up pews and giving into a pot which is distributed. I don't think that is an efficient way of getting things done and it becomes political and about a power dynamic. As a pioneer it is difficult to rely on that because you are at the mercy of the givers. I know it has worked for years and giving is part of faith. Over the last twenty years emerging communities have had to think differently. We're creative innovative thinkers so being in the playground of entrepreneurship makes sense. I have felt called to try and figure that out and stand on my own two feet or for the community to stand on its own two feet and not rely on handouts. There are lots of charities in the third sector who tick boxes to get the next handout. I've been there myself. You can get into that sector and go round and round in the washing machine.

S: It's both/and. You have to work on the value proposition if you want investment. We have to show impact. Building community costs. Usually somebody catalyses and somebody nurtures and somebody sustains. The biggest danger is that we aren't honest about the true cost and we aren't sure of the value we are providing. Sometimes money does give you some freedom too. We also need a good ecosystem to support pioneers. I don't think we have done that as well as we could.

J: Finally any tips for people starting out?

G: I was thinking about the Guinness advert from the 90s of the surfer who is waiting for the wave. In the video the guy is watching and waiting and counting and waiting for the perfect wave and he knows when that moment is and he just goes into the water and all hell breaks loose. He just catches the wave and rides it. Then you see him afterwards. The vocal behind it says 'we wait that's what we do'. In those cycles we are on the beach a lot of the time watching the waves counting them through looking for the right moment. Sometimes we go and it's not the right moment and we get wiped out and get washed up on the beach and that's ok but we dust ourselves down and go again. There are seasons. The farm has good years and bad years. At the end of the cycle we need to write it down or take on the role of reportage - to say look we've tried this, this is the learning, this is what worked and what didn't. Some things caught the wave. So for new people starting out then there is support and understanding.

B: We often use a wave analogy too. Depending on the size of the wave they sometimes need someone on a jet ski to get them up to speed. But sometimes you have to ride the wave until it ends and you don't know. We're nearly four years in - we might be here a lot longer than we originally thought!

S: The cyclical nature is so helpful - build, measure , learn. When we do look back we will see the history. The other factor is that the world keeps changing so we have to be careful to pay attention to that and not just get caught up in what we are building. Con-

"When I speak of **creativity** I am referring to **'dreamers who do'** - that is those rather rare people who are **gifted at both dreaming up the new and doing."**

Gerald Arbuckle

WORK

George Lois, a creative who designed an amazing array of big advertising campaigns says that to create great work you must spend your time as follows:

1% inspiration
9% perspiration
90% justification

(In Damn Good Advice)

There are two stages to pioneering – seeing and building. Our reflections so far have focused on the first – seeing, dreaming and imagining new possibilities which many pioneers are naturally good at. Lois calls that inspiration. In some ways that is the easy part. Equally as important is the process of building which takes effort, discipline, putting in the hours – perspiration as Lois calls it. 'Dreamers who do' is a great description for pioneers as it brings together the dreaming and the work. Lois adds a third aspect to the process and that is the effort required to justify or sell your pioneering to others which

may well be the hardest part. Lois certainly thinks so by quite a long stretch. He says it's what separates those who are consistently good from those who are some of the time.

In the survey responses this seems to be borne out. The areas pioneers identify as needing most help with are admin, managerial and other practical skills, money, and time. This is all perspiration. There was only one response where someone identified creativity as the area they needed help in.

The area named as most likely to derail pioneering is the powers that be. The top thing pioneers say they wish they knew when they were starting out is how hard it would be with the church. Two of the top things pioneers need help with are support, permission and understanding at the structural level and winning or earning trust by that same structure. These are all justification.

Lois may well be onto something.

What tools help you build your pioneering project?

A tool is something that helps you do work more easily or efficiently. So for example a spiritual practice like the examen helps you discern more easily where God is at work in your life. Asset Based Community Development helps you develop positive solutions to community issues based on things that are already present in the community. One answer to the question of what tools help was "Things theological college didn't teach me: fundraising, financial skills, networking, planning, evaluations and risk taking. Juggling complex demands and priorities was learned elsewhere than the church". That answer is really getting at something important - where pioneers have been trained in the church there is simply not a lot of practical training.

Broadly speaking the ones mentioned can be grouped into:

Spiritual practices

Research

Reflective practice

Theological reflection

Communications

Social media and technology

Community organising and development

Grant application and data gathering

Youth development

Project management

Design thinking

Evaluation

Time management

Change management

Methods or processes for developing a pioneering project over time

PEGS TO HANG A PLAN ON

There is no one approach to building a pioneering project. But it is really helpful to have a framework that can act like a series of pegs on which to hang a plan and a process. That is useful for several reasons. It helps you break it down from a big idea to something manageable. It gives you a process that you can use with others you invite into the project – the more they own it with you the better. It can help you create ways of reflecting on and indicating how it is going. When you communicate with others – supporters, funders, employers – knowing and being able to articulate what you are doing is important and gives people confidence. Here are three frameworks that you could use to plan. There are lots of others. It really helps to use something that sits well with the kind of project you are building.

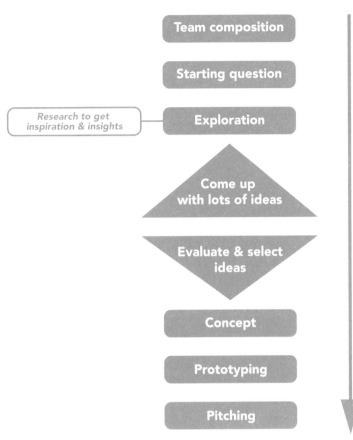

Team composition

Starting question

Research to get inspiration & insights — **Exploration**

Come up with lots of ideas

Evaluate & select ideas

Concept

Prototyping

Pitching

1. DESIGN THINKING

Design Thinking is a five-step process from innovation company IDEO. The five steps are: empathise, define, ideate, prototype, test. I like the rework of that process below that is the work of Coen Luijten and Joris van Doren in their book Creativity Works.

Team composition
Have you got one or two others who can join you for the adventure to share ideas with? It's always more fun with others.

Starting question
What is it you are longing to do something about? It might be to do with a gap, something you notice, an opportunity, a dissatisfaction.

Exploration
Gain as much insight and inspiration as you can about the question.
Do some research, find out what others do about it, read up on it, explore the situation where you are.

Come up with lots of ideas
The more ideas the better at this stage because it gives you more to play with.
Dream, brainstorm, play. However you like to do it.

Evaluate and select ideas
Sift your ideas down.
You are looking for ideas that have some sort of wow factor - they grab you and they are doable. It might be a stretch but they can be done.
Distill it down to one if you can.

Concept
The concept is simply the idea developed further.
How is it going to work?
How is it going to have legs?

Prototyping
Test the idea out and get feedback.
It doesn't need to be fully developed as the feedback will help you develop it further.
Repeat until you are ready

Pitch
Plan your launch well and set it loose in the world!
This may or may not involve a pitch.

listening

loving & serving

building community

exploring discipleship

church taking shape

doing it again

underpinned by prayer, ongoing listening and relationships with the wider church

2. FRESH EXPRESSIONS JOURNEY

In answer to the survey question how you would describe your pioneering the largest category was a church. The fresh expressions journey can be a helpful framework for that kind of pioneering.

The start point is listening. That listening is to God, prayerfully noticing where God might be at work and what God might be saying. It involves looking, noticing, observing what is going on. It involves listening to people and what they are saying. Research like doing a local survey can be a helpful way to engage and listen. It will also likely involve listening together with others on a team. Gradually you build up a picture of what you are seeing, hearing and sensing.

The next step is to love and serve. Out of what you have seen what ways can you add to the good in a place or community? This is a great way of meeting more people and doing stuff with and alongside them. Where possible it is best to join in things that already exist so you are alongside others and not in a position of leadership or power.

You don't want to start or do something on your own, so the third process is building community. This is likely with one or two others who are joining you as team in the adventure but crucially it is beginning to build community locally with others. Food is always good for this. Share in activities around local concerns. Hang out in the community. Take time to be present and meet people. Community is the seedbed for everything else really.

Through sharing life and friendships, conversations about faith will happen naturally and with those who are open and interested you can explore discipleship together in ways that make sense in that community.

Church begins to take shape and as it does you will want to create some gatherings, prayer, worship. This should all be done shaped by the culture there, not church culture from the outside. And give it time and space to breathe.

I think I'd like to add a sub-step of that last one or a further step which is about handing on the leadership to people from the local community. They know their culture best so the sooner they can lead the better and you might be ready to move on.

The whole process is undergirded by prayer. And the relationship with the wider church is always critical to get right and do as well as possible.

It is also worth noting four key features of fresh expressions as a kind of check as it develops: formational, contextual, missional, ecclesial.

3. ABCD

A community development tool that resonates with many pioneers is Asset Based Community Development. Unlike other approaches this does not focus on needs, deficits or problems. The glass is half full, not half empty. It sees a community as having many gifts, resources and assets already present. Assets are gifts that individuals bring to the table. It is a common misconception that the asset is an organisation, or structure, or even building. It is relationships-driven and believes people are the greatest resource for building stronger community. From a mission perspective God is already present too, a huge asset! Through relationships people can identify and uncover those gifts, make connections and participate together to make their community a better place to live. Rather than needing an external agency to fix them, a community is able to take responsibility for its own development. It is an inside out process rather than top down.

Patient Presencing
For it to work well, like nearly all the models here, the pioneer will need to be present in a community, listening, building friendships and letting go of their own desire to do stuff themselves, treasure seeking. If it's a community where they have lived for a long time all the better. A posture of being with and alongside the community is essential. Al Barrett calls it 'patient presencing'. This is really the first slow step.

Discovery
The second step is one of discovery. Through stories, research and community conversations and gatherings a picture can be built up of the assets in the community. There are several layers to that of individuals, groups or associations and institutions. Individual people are key – what do they have in their hearts, heads and hands? What are their passions, knowledge and skills? What groups and associations exist in the community? And are there assets through institutions – government, charity, business, faith communities? The picture that builds up should create a map of the gifts and assets of the community.

Connecting and mobilising
How can connections be made between people and groups to develop new ideas or enterprises or reimagine things to make the community better? The pioneer connects people together with space for stuff to emerge. This is different to an activist who might gather volunteers around an already semi-formed idea. Enabling a core group to emerge who can lead the process will be important. Ideas can also flow through informal connections and introductions. Every community has some natural networkers and connectors – they are key to spot and draw in. Winning hearts and minds will be helped by having one or two outcomes that people can see and feel good about. This can then move on at some stage to the creation of a community vision and plan. It is at that stage that if there are ideas that would be helped by investment or resources from outside the community they can be leveraged by the community.

For it to go well you must trust the local people and trust the process to allow things to emerge - and not be afraid to let die the things that don't hold energy. The role of the pioneer is to remove barriers, but not to do it for people or rescue ideas that are failing.

Wonderful good can come through this process. In terms of mission it's about seeing what God is doing and joining in, the kingdom coming on earth as in heaven, and simply being good news. The community focus is the whole community of which church is a part like yeast or salt which influences the whole.

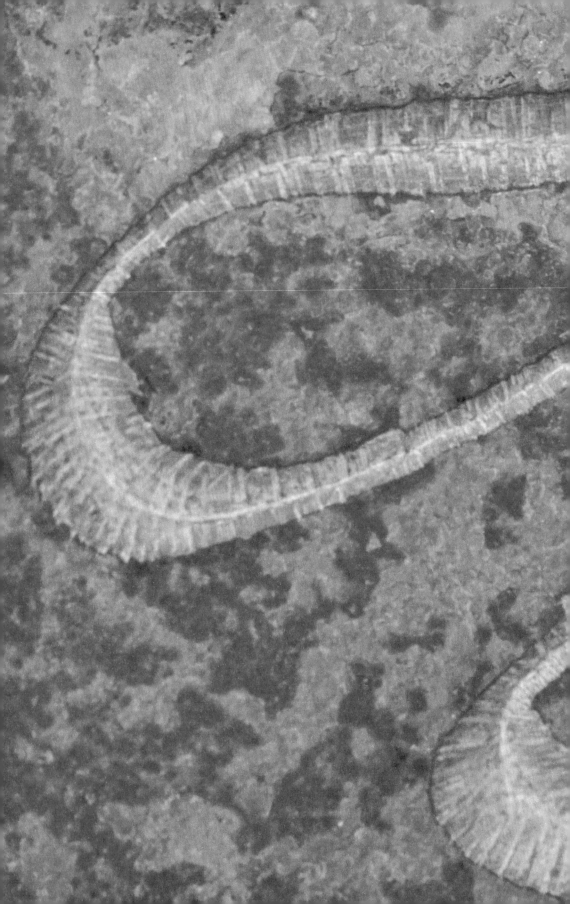

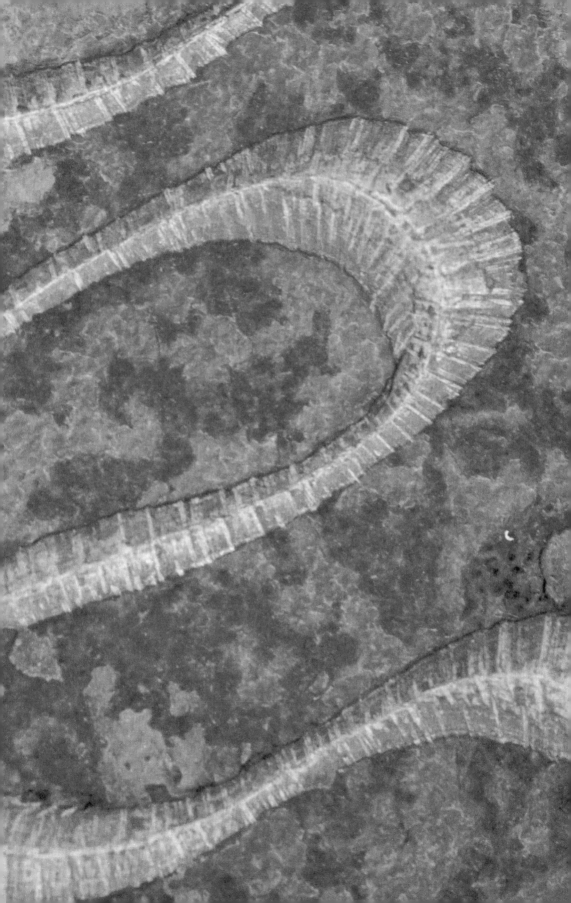

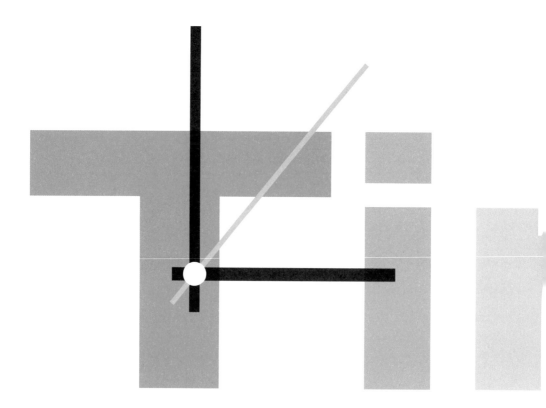

In the survey pioneers said time was one of the two biggest challenges they face. Further, lack of time is the thing most likely to derail pioneering, second only to 'the powers that be'.

How much time have you got?
There is a fairly even spilt in the survey between pioneers who are pioneering full time, part time, within other jobs and in their spare time. Depending which of these you are, the time you have available will be very different. Time though is still a challenge in all those scenarios.

So it's worth pondering:
What time do you actually have available?
What time do you have per day, week, month?
How many years do you have to give to this pioneering project?

Write it down. If you have others joining you talk with them about it.

How can you use your time well?
What is the main thing you are focused on in your pioneering? Give your best time and energy to that. Ringfence time for that. You may need to be brutal about it.

There will always be urgent things that crop up. If you keep responding to the urgent then you won't get to the important. By way of example, in the early stages of pioneering a community project, perhaps you identify hanging around in the community, being present, getting to know people is the important thing. That has to be diaried because it will never be urgent.

If you are in a part time role or split role especially if employed by a church the gravity will pull you in towards the internal agenda rather than the outward pioneering. So ringfence the time for the outward.

There will always be distractions. We live in an era of distractions. Put your phone away, ignore social media, turn off notifications. Attend to those when you choose rather than when they demand.

Make time for the important work.
Make time for admin.
Make time for creative thinking.
Make time for people.
Make time for team.
Make time for the community.
Make time for prayer, retreat and reflection.
Make time for learning.
Make time for rest, play and holiday.
Make time for the difficult things that you put off.

We are all different.
We work differently.

What suits you?
Do you do your best work in the morning
or evening?
Weave your time into a pattern or a rhythm that fits
you well.

You'll do no one any favours least of all yourself if
you burn out. So pace yourself. Get a balance in
your life of work and play and rest. Have some other
interests in your life that you give time to so you
switch off from work.

How long does pioneering take?

It takes longer than you think! That is the wisdom
from pioneers in answer to the question of what
they know now that they wish they knew when they
started.

There are so many kinds of pioneering it is hard to
generalise but we have deliberately included timelines in the stories throughout. From the initial tug
of the heart strings through to a complete cycle of
setting it up and developing a community and getting to succession took the Upper Room 15 years.

The social or missional enterprise shaped projects typically seem to take about three years
from the initial working on the idea to launch
– that was the case with Home Cafe and Clean
for Good. In the background has often been

the percolating of an idea for longer than that
working on a slow hunch. Then perhaps there is
another three-year window to navigate to stability.
If it's a side project this length of time is potentially
longer.

For those pioneering in mission in a community, network or housing area to share the
story of Jesus and to help build a better world, if
that is a new context the received wisdom from
the fresh expressions journey is that this process takes about eight to ten years if it is in a
genuinely new context rather than one where
relationships had already been built. In mission in new cultures and languages overseas this
process sometimes would take 30 years!

In Sue Steer's case there have been about three
years of listening, presence, building relationships,
experimenting, adapting and community is growing. Prior to that was a longer process of the idea
and developing the project through Churches Together which probably was a five-year process. That
has now got to the stage where all sorts of things
have been catalysed through that initial patient
work.

The Boxing Church launched as a congregation after three years but began the boxing club ▶

within one. But David was already present in that community and had the time and money to be able to do it.

A new congregation or church plant can be quicker. It might take a year or two to work on the plan, build a team and do the ground work. Then there will be a season of patient further work to develop the life of the new church, connect with those outside, introduce new people to faith and disciple those that want to pursue it further, and hopefully nurture leaders and pioneers who will catalyse further new things.

When it comes to finding some depth in a new community, that too takes more time than you think. Roy Searle who is one of the key people in the Northumbria Community reflects that a community is only really ready to reflect on its values or ethos after about ten years. There is an issue of depth here – you only find depth in relationships over time which is slow work.

This issue of how much time it takes is important to bear in mind in relation to funding. If it's a side project it's not generally an issue. Where start-up money is secured for a salary for pioneering it is typical for that to be for a three-year period. That is helpful but depending on the kind of project, it is unlikely to have developed into something self- sustaining so it is worth considering resolving that conundrum is part of the pioneering work. An alternative might be to stretch to six years half-time funding instead and work for the other half in another job, or commit to raise half the funds in another way.

When is it time for a pioneer to move on?
There is no right answer to this. But there are probably two risks:

The first is to leave too quickly and think that the work is done. In Do Purpose, David Hieatt suggests asking yourself three questions:

Do you still love it?
Is it still fun?
Is the job only half done?

If the answer is yes to these three then keep building. Certainly in Ann-Marie's case of campaigning to end FGM she has committed to stay in the fight for example. In our culture it's assumed it makes sense to keep moving on but that isn't always the best thing to do.

The second risk is too stay too long. By doing so you may stop the development of local leadership for example. This is as much about posture as it is about time perhaps and is where having some nous about issues of cross cultural mission can be invaluable.

I have worked for CMS for 18 years. It's almost embarrassing to say it in our culture. In that time, I have been passionate about catalysing creative approaches to mission and encouraging them. The pioneer training which I pioneered is now ten years in at the point of writing. I have restructured it to pass on the leading of Oxford Centre so I am free to develop other aspects of the vision. But I can answer yes to all three questions above so as best I can discern it still feel I should be pioneering where I am. I have asked other people to tell me when it is time for me to leave because it is also possible to delude ourselves.

Money

Talking about money is hard. I don't know why but most of us are not good at it. We love creativity and ideas. We love sailing off the edge and carving a new way. We love making new connections. We're passionate about making a difference. But the maths? that can wait can't it?!

Our survey showed that money is not the driver for you. 94% of you would choose freedom rather than be controlled because of money. If you are pioneering to make money you should probably just go and run a business selling some stuff instead. But equally money was one of the things that you said was most challenging and most likely to derail your pioneering.

The basic question is pretty simple:
How will you resource your pioneering project?

Step 1 is asking that question early on in a project and not putting it off.

Step 2 is accepting that no one else is likely to do that work for you. Money will not fall out of the sky. So don't wait around for someone else to fix it and don't moan about it. No one owes you anything!

Step 3 is then doing the required thinking, planning and maths. That will be affected by the sort of pro-

ject it is and the kind of structure you might need. So it is worth taking time to think that through and develop a plan. However simple the project is that plan should have a budget with some income and expenditure over time which will probably be best guesses.

Step 4 For some of us the idea of a budget or spreadsheet is not what we are good at. So it may help to get someone in the team who does that well. You are well on the way if you are thinking and planning and getting a team who can do that with you. When I set up the CMS pioneer training I asked for help writing a business plan and someone sent me some examples and talked me through what it should include.

Step 5 is then putting the plan into action which is the work as much as sailing off the edge. It will be a good chance to test the vision and plan by sharing it with others especially if you are asking them to get behind it with you. It may also require setting up a structure. And there are of course no guarantees when you are making a new path so it may require some adapting as you go.

▶

While there can be various approaches there is quite a bit of thinking around at the moment that a good way to start is by developing something small that you can get started as leanly as possible. Initially it can be a side project. Then as it grows it can then attract more funding and income and you can increase capacity. CMS founders had two principles along these lines – 'start small' and 'money follows vision'. One of the simplest ways to fund pioneering in other words is to keep your day job and grow pioneering slowly on the side.

The stories in Pioneer Practice show a range of structures and funding models.

Boxing Community – David was initially funded by his local church to pioneer and does so now as a Pioneer Curate paid for by the diocese. He is expected to do other things as well in that job so it's part of a mix.

FGM – Ann Marie Wilson took her vision to various organisations. She became a mission partner with CMS supported by churches and individuals. She was housed in one charity and has now set up 28toomany as a charity in its own right with a mix of individual donations and grants.

Clean for Good – This is an enterprise and required a business plan, a board of directors and initial investment to around 100k from stakeholders/partners. It has grown into a sustainable business employing around 40 cleaners.

Sacred Bean – Jo and Darren are employed by the Methodist Church pioneering with the local community and those at the edge. This created the space to develop Sacred Bean as a social enterprise under that umbrella. Income generated will pay the workers. But it is a mix of church support for Jo and Darren and enterprise income for others. The plan is it becomes sustainable as a business.

Cherish has been developed as a side project by Erika. So far money has come from grants and the local church to pay the design and print costs of material. There are as yet no salary costs. The course material will generate income once up and running as others buy into it.

Lubbesthorpe community was funded by Churches Together with a vision for pioneering in a New Housing project. After initial funding for three years it has been renewed but there is a plan for diversification of income from developer money, grants, and members of the community with a tapering off of Churches Together investment.

Home Cafe was developed by Meg putting huge amounts of time in to the plan and stopping other work to do so. She and her family lived off her partner's salary during that time. They raised some grant funding to kickstart it. Then it has a model to be a sustainable enterprise which it is just about breaking even on. But it does have volunteer help to run.

Upper Room reaches a group of people right on the edge with no money or potential for income. It is a charity and has been funded through fundraising for grant-based income. This has included some diocesan funding including a period when Kim was being trained and then a pioneer curate.

The structures range from voluntary group, charity in own right, under umbrella of a wider charity, social enterprise, support as missionary, community interest company, church project under wider umbrella. Income is a mix of patronage, individual giving, grants, enterprise for services and goods, church and mission budgets (supported through giving). From our survey the majority of pioneer projects are community projects and new forms of church. So they are most likely resourced through charities, individual giving and grants or being done in peoples spare time as side projects.

Do the maths!

Team

The stereotype the word pioneer conjures up is of a lone individual. This is really unhelpful! Pioneering sometimes starts that way but it definitely goes best when there is a team involved. That team might be as small as two or three people but it is definitely easier and more fun when a load is shared and there are people to knock ideas around with. Teams are made up of people so they are alive, dynamic, organic and there are no hard and fast rules about what makes them work well. That's part of the adventure.

In the early stages of pioneering when there is simply the idea, one of the best things to do is to talk about it. It helps you develop and test the idea to say it out loud. Start with close friends and people you trust to gauge reaction but then talk about it more widely. That is a good way of seeing who sparks off it, who lights up and who comes towards you. That way you begin to build up a group who are interested and who are caught by the vision. Then somewhat counter intuitively slow down! It's easy to get over excited at this point and invite everyone into the project because of your enthusiasm but that might create problems down the line. So pause and reflect. What is important for your core team? What do you want and need and what do they want and need?

Three areas worth thinking about in that pause are alignment, personality and expectations.

Are you all passionate about the vision and aligned on it? When you have an idea there is a process to go through of refining it and really distilling your why, your purpose. There are various tools you could use to think about that - mission, vision and values is one. Finding your why is another. Exploring that together with your fledgling team is a great way to test that fit. It may be something you have already done in which case share that and see if others are on board and aligned to it or not.

Any team needs a mix of gifts and skills and personalities. In Erika's story she found people with particular skills she needed and didn't have. There are various tools out there related to personality - myers briggs, enneagram, strength finders are three I have used. They can be really helpful for teams. Difference is good. You don't want a team of people exactly like you. People have baggage or issues - that may be to do with life circumstances, anxiety, mental health. So when you put your team together try and discern where people are at. When you are in a start up situation you don't want too many people who will require lots of energy and attention. So go in with your eyes open as best you can.

Then thirdly it is really worth exploring expectations.

What are you all in it for - money, a job, satisfaction, profile, ego, the difference the project will make? What outcomes are you expecting? Is it a volunteer or paid role? If so how many hours? And are there expectations around church culture that need exploring? If it's a new mission project do you expect people to make your project the main thing or is it fine if they go to their own church as well? You get a clash of expectations when pioneers are assuming they will grow something reflecting the local culture but volunteers are not aware of that expectation and are attached to particular ways of doing church and associated theologies. You don't want to be too heavy about this but it's far better to name things than leave them hidden to surface later.

Teams move through phases. The early age of shaping the idea and getting it started tends to have a lot of energy in it and is done by a close knit small group. It can be the most work but is also fun. As it grows inevitably it moves into a phase where there will be a wider circle of people involved as volunteers. There can be some significant change points related to structure. For example for Ann Marie Wilson the point at which a charity is set up for 28toomany required volunteers in trustee roles. That creates a whole new layer of team with considerable power so needs careful navigation. Clean For Good's core team of four making things happen had to change to develop a business with new team roles on a board and employing staff. Ben Thorpe's loose community meeting in homes eating together needed different roles when they moved to meeting in a public space and so on. Perhaps the widest

circle is those interested in the project who want to know how it's going and cheer you on and stay informed. Building an email list and regular communication will prove invaluable over time. There is a particularly tricky team challenge in cross-cultural mission for those pioneering a community of disciples where there hasn't been one. That goes best when leadership moves into the hands of those who are insiders to that culture or else it will remain foreign and never properly take root there. A goal in that scenario is for the team to change and for those involved initially to take a back seat or plan to exit eventually. There are no hard and fast rules to any of this but it's not as simple as creating a team and you are done. It's helpful to think of the layers of team and of their levels of participation and helping those various layers thrive. And it's helpful to think how team moves and shifts over time especially at significant change points and be ready for bumps in the road that creates.

How can you create space for the team to thrive, flourish and grow? I think about this as the air a team breathes. There are some basic things that can be easy to miss especially if there's work to get on with. Everyone likes to be appreciated, thanked, noticed, trusted, seen, heard, given responsibility. They don't like being checked up on, controlled, micro managed. The team is the work as much as the work is the work so give time to it and the people in it both individually and together as team and be fully present. Create space to be together in ways that aren't always task focused. Food is always good. Make it a fun team to be part of.

Community

Paul Bradbury

In this over-individualised world there is a thirst for community. However, those who seek it find it hard to realise. Bonhoeffer said that Christian community ultimately is a gift. He said that if you love the dream or vision of community more than Christian community itself you won't realise the dream.

In thinking about building community I've recently been really helped by the concept of wilding which is a radical new approach taking the world of conservation by storm. Conservation has generally taken a very human-led approach of managing the survival or reintroduction of endangered species. It's an approach that has a very specific vision and aim. Wilding on the other hand is about creating the kind of environment where biodiversity becomes possible and then seeing what happens. It's about taking our hands off the process and allowing nature to lead. In the same way with the gift of community, it's not something we can manage. But we are invited to create the kind of environment in which Christian community can flourish. It may look very different to our vision or dream. But all dreams have to die, and when they do they become seeds of something similar but infinitely richer than what we had imagined.

Our vision for Christian community in Poole was of a core network of Christians living close to one another in an area at the centre of Poole. We planned to share a rhythm of prayer and a 'Rule of Life'. We would practice the Kingdom together in different ways such as car sharing and food cooperatives. We would be in and out of one another's homes. We would be church 24/7, not just once a week on a Sunday. Others would be drawn to our life together and perhaps some of those would want to know more about the faith that inspired it.

Having started with ten adults over ten years ago we are now a community of around 50 people. We have a rhythm of prayer, a Rule of Life, but we are dispersed widely across the town and our plans for car sharing and food cooperatives never took off. We've done a whole host of things; restored a play park, run a community café, hosted a community garden, held a monthly film club, offered a space for creativity and Christian spirituality in a local café. Some have lasted, others had their time and have stopped. New things are always emerging. It's not about the projects but the relationships they enable and the opportunities they offer for transformation. Something beautiful has grown here over the years. It has always felt fragile and uncertain. It is constantly evolving. There is a wildness to it which is both terrifying and exciting.

It's tricky to offer a 'how to…' for building community. A recipe for Christian community might have

▶

ingredients but the method's a bit unreliable. So here at least is a tentative list of ingredients from our experience. These are what you might look to ensure are part of the environment that will make a rich experience of Christian community in a particular context possible.

Prayer and a 'way of life'

At its heart we sought to be people living out the way of Jesus together in our daily lives in a particular place. We drew on the descriptions of the early church and monastic tradition from Benedict onwards. There's no need to overcomplicate things. A simple rhythm of prayer that is realistic and yet committed. A set of values that sum up, from your study, reflection and conversation, the call you feel as community to live out the way of Jesus together. Write them down. Communicate them constantly and creatively so that people begin to live them naturally and wildly!

Nodes of connection (within)

A community is the sum of the flow of relationships and connections among a section of society. Some of those connections will happen spontaneously but without some sort of framework to enable community to grow it may wither before it really gets going. For us these connecting points have oriented around a rhythm of Sunday gatherings, some of which involve gathered worship, others engaging with the community. There are meals at key times of the year, regular places where people meet to pray and explore discipleship together. A key element is to take a check on the extent to which the framework of connection for community might be too heavy. Is the energy needed to try and enable community actually wearing everyone out? Time and

time again I have had to remember that the value and richness of relationship is the currency of community, not number or frequency of attendance.

Nodes of connection (without)

We have sought to be a missional community here in Poole by seeing our common life as missional in itself. So connections within and without blur and blend. We aim to serve our wider community through the gift of neighbourliness and solidarity. In practice that might mean litter picking a local beach once a month, or starting a 'street association', or creating a community allotment. All these projects are collaborative ventures with local people in which members of our community have been a part.

Unanxious and organic leadership

Leadership of an emerging community can hardly be directive. We trust that with the right elements, perseverance, prayer and the gift of time something far more rich and wild than anything we could have constructed by directive or design will emerge. Leadership must be patient, lacking anxiety, drive or the need to be at the centre of everything. It must know when there is nothing more to do than nothing, that knows when it's time to sleep, that sleep does not imply that nothing is happening. A leadership that focusses on processes not results, on the environment for growth not growth itself.

At the end of his book After Virtue, Alasdair MacIntyre, says 'we are waiting…for another – doubtless very different – St Benedict.' I agree. We have lost the art and value of community when we so clearly need it. And it will take the passionate and patient commitment of pioneers to imagine, experiment and explore ways of building it again in the post-Christian west.

The Desert

It goes by many names – darkness, chaos, desert, liminality, the wilderness, Gethsemane, the dark forest. But the journey to the new invariably seems to go through this place. It would be much easier all round if it was possible to jump from the old to the new in one sweet move with no pain. But it rarely is.

It's a place of being stripped of certainty.
A place of insecurity.
A place of unknowing.
A place where you have let go of the old but you can't yet see the way ahead.
A place of self-doubt.
A place where your internal critic goes into overdrive.

A place where you feel like giving up.
A place of wondering why on earth you embarked on this journey.

It can also be a creative place.
A place of learning.
A place for deep questions about who you are and what you are about.
A place that shapes you.
A place to be silent and listen.
A place you are alone with God.
A place of prayer.
A place of new resolve.

If you find yourself in that place it's normal.
Try not to run from it too quickly.

"...this beautiful world with everything set right, free from brokenness, creation healed."

Change ➡

God's dream, the kingdom of God is this beautiful world with everything set right, free from brokenness, creation healed. As pioneers we are gripped by that dream of another possible world and seek to join with God's Spirit in playing a part in bringing change now while we also anticipate a different future. At one level it's simple – the anger or dissatisfaction we have with what is not working enables us to imagine and build something that makes a difference. That's what we're good at! But as time goes by other questions surface – what is the best way of making that change with the time and energy and resources we have? How do you know what difference you are making and is it possible to demonstrate or measure it? That can be important at least for those we are accountable to and communicate with. Then invariably we meet resistance from the powers that be. Sometimes that resistance feels wilful and at others times it's just because the culture or the system is stacked a particular way. So acting to change the world leads you to having to consider how to navigate and bring change in wider structures, systems, cultures. It is striking in the research how often pioneers name the challenges of navigating, being understood and being derailed by those in power in the structures they operate in. Any read of prophets is a poignant reminder that it has always been thus. How do you stay true and keep going when it gets really hard? It's not good to be isolated that's for sure - connecting with others in networks and as part of a wider movement is how the world gets changed. The world itself is changing rapidly so pioneers need to be adaptive and flexible to ride those changes in the wider environment.

What tactics have you learned about change...

These themes have been distilled and collated from the answers to the survey question above. They are not individual answers, but put together there is so much practical wisdom here.

The new belongs elsewhere. Find space at the edges or under the radar or in parallel rather than trying to change existing structures. Avoid being too visible. Affirm those in existing structures so the new is not a threat but part of a mixed economy.

Prioritise pioneering practice on the ground that people can see, that demonstrates it works. Start small, prove your track record then upscale. It helps to point out other case studies and stories. Give time to the pioneering work – make that the focus. Don't get too drawn into the wider structures as they will take your time and energy.

Share what you are doing, communicate, tell stories, keep everyone informed, talk about what you are doing as normal not weird, explain why change is needed as clearly as possible, and don't assume people have understood.

Build trust, relationships and favour slow and steady with church, council, developer and other stakeholders. Treat speaking their language in the same way you do the community you are pioneering with i.e. as cross-cultural, so learn their political language and speak in ways and categories they get.

...within wider structures or systems?

Collaborate where possible. Build a guiding coalition. Find people/ friends in the structures who are for you and pioneering, who are authority dissenters. It's easy to think your pioneering is enough but real change comes with both pathfinding dissent and authority dissent working together.

Write down vision and expectations and get them agreed early on by stakeholders. The earlier the better. This will be important when resistance comes. There will be resistance. Expect it. Be tactical. Know when to wait, when to work round, when to be subversive, when to bring in an outside respected voice on pioneering.

Be nice, humble, kind, loving, patient. When people write difficult emails take the time to reply graciously. But also be persistent, dogged and deter- mined pursuing what needs to be done. Stay true; don't crave approval.

Some are called to wider systemic change. For that pioneers or pioneer enablers are helpful at different levels of structures. Being bi-lingual is an essential skill. In those structures there is a time to name the elephant in the room, a time to be silent, a time to give space to grieve for the old, and a time to claim the tradition over and against itself. Know what time it is.

PRAY

A SLOW RISE

ANNA HEMBURY

Chris and I moved to Hull in the late 90s and have lived in the Hessle Road/Boulevard area for over 20 years now. It is in the top 3% of poorest everything and is the sort of place most people avoid. We both felt called to incarnational mission - just being present, living alongside and serving the community. There's something about the specificity of place of the incarnation that is important. To understand a place, you've got to live in it. Isaiah 58 has been our vision - that passage about a call to the broken hearted and oppressed, to see broken places renewed. All very noble. One year in we were like 'this is so hard but these are the marvellous things we are going to do'. Five years in it was 'shit, we haven't got a clue!' At ten 'we can't go on'. You have to go through those phases. But the longer you live it out the more you get it.

I was asked how you change a place like this. It's an impossible question really. And who are we to say anyway?! But here are a few things we have learned.

You start by changing yourself and then carry on changing yourself - that's the beginning, middle and end of it.

Then you need to pay attention - attend to what's going on with people, with the neighbourhood. But it's also an intuitive listening - to what the Spirit is saying, what people are not saying, what they are really saying, and to yourself.

It takes a long time to get under the skin of a place. There is something about the length of time that is essential. Relationships of trust are built and lived out in real time. You can't short circuit the experience. We are on the third generation of kids coming through the breakfast club. Some of those we have had relationships with for 20 odd years. Others we knew well and lost touch and then they reappear. So we have learnt not to panic. The fact we have known them for that length of time means everything. It's like making bread - the best bread is slow bread - the slow rise.

I think of what we do as curating ordinary spaces of change. We've never had a plan beyond being here with people - it's easy to patronisingly do things to people or for people. Most of the things we have started evolved organically, and we take care to let things find expression more as ordinary life-as-it-should-be than extraordinary project. A couple of examples:

I felt compelled to make possible a therapeutic space where women from all walks of life could build connection, because of my relationship with women in survival sex work on the street. I asked everyone who I thought knew better than me, and they all advised against it! But I decided I had to do it anyway. I just started Orts in my house until I figured something out. Orts are "waste scraps" - and describes this women's sewing collective: a community working with discarded scraps of

▶

fabric, where women who often feel like scraps are brought together and made into something beautiful. We started Orts in my dining room with one person. Liane, who started it with me, took Orts to the CMS Make Good course to develop the idea. Very soon we got use of a room in the parish hall over the road. Now, six years in, even those who thought it risky and unprofessional, and me unqualified, think it's a good thing. Orts is a safe space for women where we can build each other up, support each other, flourish together. Spirituality is very much part of it. We have women of all faiths and none. It's a small piece of the kingdom of God. People are used to defining themselves according to a particular story and Orts gives space for their story to take a different path or for them to redefine what their story is.

We do something on a Friday at Selby St Methodist mission. I think of it as sofa church. People can eat toast, drink tea, fall asleep on a sofa, work in the garden. At some point we sit around and use a liturgy and maybe sing a song we can all sing (often Bob Marley!), we say some prayers, we cook lunch and eat together. All very ordinary. We break bread and figure out life together. A lot of those who come are homeless, have mental health problems, addictions. It's warm. They get fed. They can sleep. Over time you see people who begin very much beyond the edge, and where they park themselves slowly changes and they come in a bit closer - another slow rise - community, connection, breaking isolation. Orts and the other spaces we

curate offer a consistent presence and connection with an ever evolving spaciousness. Room for ourselves. Room for each other. Room for God.

Occasionally we find ourselves in change in the wider landscape. I ended up in a group with some of the women involved in street sex work, taking the council to court. It's not my natural environment, though I can do it - I'm better at the edge. They had imposed a social banning order, against national police guidelines. We tried to meet with the council and police and point out why it made vulnerable people more vulnerable. But we were taken round the houses, so in the end we took them to court. But then out of that one of the judge's decisions was that they needed to consult with us. They began very reluctantly, but it's swung round and now the council are asking us to shape the policy! Living here, we can build relationships with those most on the margins and then make space together for them to lead change. People on the margins have the most to teach the rest of us about what is wrong because they are the ones at the brunt end of the system. So they need to able to speak into the thing.

To make slow bread, you use very little yeast, but you need a lot more time to ferment the dough before you bake it. The bread is tastier, keeps longer and it's easier for your body to digest and absorb the nutrients. Doing life in Hull has been like this. The slow rise allows us to find rich nutrients in this written-off place, to be nourished as

"The bread is tastier, keeps longer and it's easier for your body to digest and absorb the nutrients."

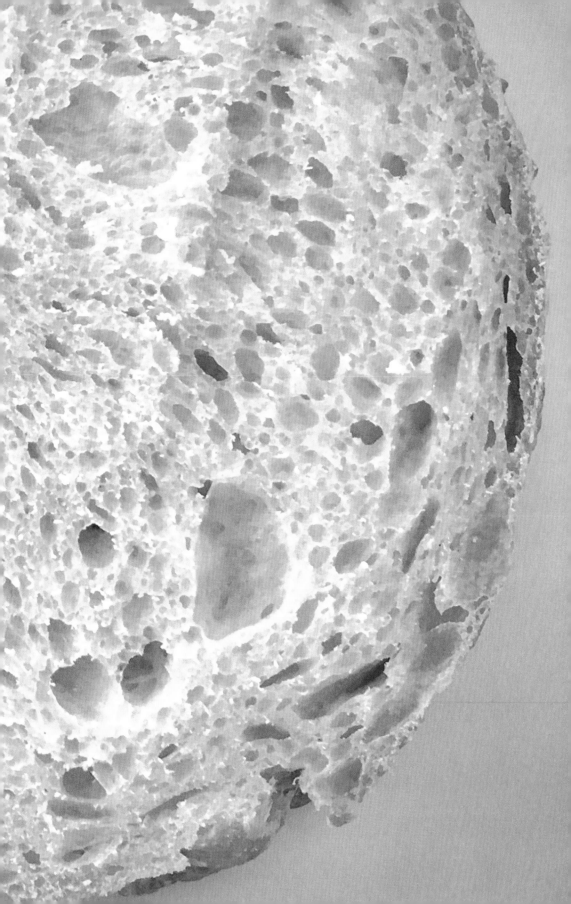

A conversation about

Tina, Ann-Marie and Richard are all involved in change which involves working with, in and navigating systems and structures. Ann-Marie Wilson is the Founder and Director of the charity 28toomany whose goal is to see an end to female genital mutilation (FGM) in 28 countries in Africa. Richard Passmore is the Northern Mission Centre Director in Carlisle Diocese. Tina Hodgett is the Evangelism and Pioneer Team Leader in Bath and Wells Diocese, though perhaps better known as the leader of the Holy Rumpus.

J: What change do you want to see?

T: I think the 'how does change happen?' question starts with God... who is the God you have encountered and how does this determine your framing of reality? I met a God who was so much more beautiful than I imagined, and much more vast and increasingly mysterious whose ways couldn't be known. This fundamentally altered my understanding of reality. Another world is not only possible but exists as an adjacent reality (the kingdom). That's the change I imagine and see - the walls of the church building coming down... the people of God connecting with the world in creative, playful, joyful ways with no pressure for 'results', allowing the Divine Council to reveal what is in their sole imagination that is beyond our imaginings and for all of that to contribute to the healing of individuals, communities, countries and the world. I long for church culture and structures to incorporate and be incorporated by the values of the kingdom, enabling the medium to be the message, for the gospel to reach into places it hasn't reached before and to sub-cul-

tures...for radical inclusivity, contextual communities arising from open, imaginative cross-cultural mission, for the church to give itself to the Spirit of God.

A: The big goal remains the global eradication of FGM. I always said it would take 12 years for a girl to not be cut to then have the mother not cut her and then after 24 to be a grandmother and not cut her so you are talking about three generations for change to really be effected. It may take 60 years. I set a ten year period in the charity I set up and we set this goal for change of ten ten ten - which is ten percent reduction in ten countries in ten years. I think we'll reach our target, and some.

R: Our vision is simple - God for all Cumbria.

J: These kinds of changes don't sound easy to pull off. Can you say something about your story and sense of call to what you are doing? Can we start with you Richard? I was surprised when you said to me that you were sensing from God that your next role was to be one in an institution or church structures because you have always been quite anarchic.

R: I think that sense of call to it was absolutely massive and I wouldn't have done it otherwise and I wouldn't have survived without that sense of call because it's been so important to still be my kind of anarchic self. That being me is absolutely key in all these spaces.

A: I had got to 40 and I met God in a significant

CHANGE

way. I had done everything I wanted to do in life so I volunteered in Africa with a charity called Medair. A year or so in I was in West Darfur which was a war zone so it was straight in the deep end and I met a little girl who had FGM at five and had been raped at ten and the whole of her village and her family had been killed and her village burned. She was left for dead but pregnant. We gave her a safe delivery. There she was with a baby at 11 years old and I looked at this child with a child and cried out to God and said "this just is not right - who is going to look after other girls like this?" because she was going to be sold off as a fourth wife to some distant cousin the other side of Sudan. And I heard God say "you will" and it was like "No I don't think so really! I am a white British HR manager from London, not an African black midwife or doctor - look at your HR department God!" I came back and spoke to my church and told them I had found out what I was meant to do - eradicate FGM across Africa.

J: Tina you were pioneering in Portishead and jumped into a diocesan role to effect change. How did that come about?

T: When the team leader role came up I was pressed strongly to apply. I went on retreat having said no I didn't want to do it, I didn't believe in evangelism. But on retreat I sat down and talked to God seriously about it and had this light sound experience connecting five different things from my past which were about setting people free. These images came and came so I thought I'd better apply for it. But I said in the application – I am offering myself but I've been sent with a particular mission. What I am here

to do is… and I had four points. I was kind of saying I don't care if you give me the job or not but this is what I'll do if you appoint me. Lo and behold they did.

J: How on earth do you go about developing a strategy to end FGM?

A: I took seven years to prepare. I went to Pakistan and learned midwifery. I went to Nigeria and learned about fistular surgery and what happens when FGM has gone wrong or when FGM has happened and girls can't give safe delivery. I completed a psychology doctorate, I did a number of courses and went to Interhealth and eventually ticked the boxes to get a certificate to say I was psychologically ok, fit for global travel. I found CMS who took me on as a mission partner and spent a further year to figure out what I was doing and test out my ideas, visit CMS Africa, other charities, find some funding, build a team of volunteers including one who had just left a law firm and so on. And I looked around at what other people were doing.

But for the strategy I borrowed someone's house for three days and with flip charts and post it notes wrote and stuck everything round the room I could think of and wrote it up. I then sent it to half a dozen bright strategy type people to see what they thought and they said it looks good. One said you are further ahead in year one than we were in year ten. It must have been a God thing. I had this idea of a pincer approach. You start with the top and push down - you want the first ladies, the Pope,

▶

"I look harmless as a petite woman from London. That's a tactic because I am a lot more harm than people think...

the Archbishops, the UN. Then you also start at the other end, the grassroots and you have to convince the NGOs, what do they need on the ground and you squeeze the problem from both angles. So the top lot push the resources to the right people. By helping the top you also help the grassroots NGOs. By helping the 'bottom' they stand behind us and trust what we say is going on and get it spoken about in millennial goals or General Synod or whatever.

So pushing from both ends has been my strategy and if you look up our theory of change on our web site you will see it there.

And then data and research is the other part of the strategy. We aimed to do 28 country reports and will do that, yet we realised we had to do law reports as well so will have done 28 of those. And we have done thematic reports on things like medicalisation, social norms, and we're doing one on faith, on diaspora, one on stats because they cover the whole 28 laterally as well as deep and narrow. We aim to be the portal, the Google of the sector. But we simply have to show what is going on with great clarity and understanding and interpretation.

Then we are aware that what we are dealing with is culture change so our report on social norms and FGM maps that out and offers a strategic approach for how to work at the grassroots or local level in community dialogue at the various levels. That is so important too.

J: I was so impressed when I read that report - that shows the depth to which what you are dealing with involves culture change. Richard within four years or so you have generated the situation that one in four people in Cumbria in a community of disciples are in a fresh expression of church. It's amazing really. How have you gone about that?

R: Two things were in place - a vision 'God For

All' in Cumbria and a permission giver or authority dissenter in the Bishop who appointed me. Those were critical. The maximum reach of the church is about 5-15% because the church relies on networks of family and friends reaching out to people they know. Much of my early work was around developing practice on the ground to reach beyond that. This included third space fresh expressions that were deliberately not connected with churches. These were set up to be pathfinders, to constructively disrupt, to be innovative, to playfully push the boundaries, challenging the status quo both in terms of thinking and practice. Two examples of this are Mountain Pilgrims and Maranatha Yoga. The growth of these early developments made clear the need to invest in developing work with people outside of the structures and possible cultural reach of church as we know it. An increasingly pressing question was how to foster an appropriate space and climate for pioneering to thrive that benefits both traditional church and those outside. So that too is part of our strategy. The challenge ahead is how to not only nurture the breadth of growth but establish a depth to the pioneer charism that is sparking into life, and nurture discipleship within fresh expressions. Then we have developed other fresh expressions closer to the church's understanding and have created communities of practice or networks around them to encourage others that they too can start new things.

I have had a very clear theory of change in the background of what I am doing which is to constructively disrupt business as usual through transparent operations and real relationships. The church knows it's on a burning platform and it's got to change but unless you give them a vision of the future they can't step into the new thing. So I try and use that creatively. The transparent operation increases your impact because you can see and learn from other people. The real relationships increase your capacity on the ground. I have also used a lot of the language the church knows and uses - statistics, strategy and so on which has been helpful. The statistic

...yet by the time they realise, it's too late!"

you mentioned has been pretty helpful in showing what is happening, that the strategy is bearing fruit.

J: Tina how did you go about developing a strategy for newness and change within diocesan structures?

T: The strategy and doing is important and I am always impressed by Richard and we of course have developed that and have a plan to appoint ten pioneers (we're up to six) and actually a similar plan with networks related to types of practice, and are trying to create a different air that people breathe, and have a hub with CMS to encourage and train people. But to take a different tack, my strategy has been being myself (and people call me bonkers and crazy) - I have just resisted conformity and the pressure to accept the status quo and the apparent boundaries of possibility. Then I've also gone somewhere else, created a new place. My place is the world of metaphor and that's a new land so you don't talk in any of the existing language, you create metaphor and you make people talk in a different space altogether. I try and talk in poetry and not prose because there is much more possibility in it - I love the poem by Emily Dickinson 'I dwell in possibility". That's where I live. I invent my own language and don't use the old language. I talk about Holy Rumpus, God-talk, God-life, the Divine Council (the trinity). My office is called the dreamerie. If you are using different language you are disrupting the existing norms. I am also a role model. It is like, oh there is someone in the diocese who says all this sort of stuff can happen. I'm there speaking out new things. And others are going "ooooh I'd like to go there".

J: In the research with pioneers when we asked what was most likely to derail pioneering the number one answer was the powers that be. When we asked what they need help with, support and understanding in church structures was second. Our learning with pioneers over the last ten years is that the journey to the new always

goes through difficulty. It's hard to say why that should be the case. Maybe it's as simple as being a threat because you see and propose something different and that rattles the cage. In the case of the church it's odd because you think surely the church knows it needs to change and pioneers are both essential and a great gift?! What's been your engagement with the powers that be?

T: I work next to Wells Cathedral and it is a symbol in my mind of all the structures. And if you think about trying as one person to move that building that is what it feels like. But obviously it's God's work... and credit where it's due, the Diocese made space for the newness to happen and that does feel like a gift.

Working in the diocesan structures though was a journey of frustration most of the time. Year one was about trying to understand and withstand the cultural pressures and the status quo. Year two was slowly identifying allies at grassroots, investing in them and bringing them on board. Then year 3 felt as though there was more energy in the system - people keep using the words excitement and energy in relation to pioneers. It was great to see in the research on tactics that pioneers recognise the need for permission givers or authority dissenters in the system as Richard mentioned. I have two or three and one of them has been great – when I was writing one section of the Strategic Development Fund bid he said 'Have you said everything you wanted to say?' which is possibly the best question anyone has ever asked me in a work context. But either they don't have enough power...or they have been half permission givers! It's like they can't quite bring themselves to set you free. There was one point where I had seven lines of accountability.

A: In Nigeria I experienced the most difficulty. This was in my preparation phase. I was sent out by the parent charity to get the daughter charity fund raise

▶

ready. When I got there it was a facade. I bust a gut to get it shaped up but the project manager I was trying to change found me a threat. I heard from the office manager that her sons had said "shall we just take her out?" That's scary because that is an overt death threat. Then I was locked in a house for a few months. I couldn't tell anyone because there was no internet.

Since training as a Lay Pioneer Minister, it's sad to say but I have been very blocked by my own church, possibly because I am a woman, possibly because I am bright, so that's disappointing. It is annoying and has worn me out over the years.

The UN has bureaucracy and a lot of power. They have a lot of money slushing around and will wine and dine Muslim clerics and tell them how bad FGM is but it doesn't make much difference. They don't actually want anyone to show them the facts and this is the difficulty when we're giving them data of what is working and what isn't.

Then you have got the Grandmas who are doing it and they have status in the community which is about culture change and the economic power. The chiefs go into that category too because they often get a back hander - a cut of the cutting fee. Then there are the men who deny it all but play the field and go for a cut woman because she is chaste. As a woman it's difficult. That's why I finished my doctorate so I was an educated woman and can say I have studied FGM, culture and Islamics and know that's not right.

And then I have had difficulty with governance and team members closer to home.

R: It's hard! It has actually got more difficult as we get closer to a tipping point maybe because it's a more visible threat? I have had the equivalent of your difficult board members. At one level you think they should get it but they seem to feel threatened. And it's hard to navigate that storm.

J: It's strangely reassuring to hear that the difficulty is normal! I guess you learn some resil- ience and some tactics to help you navigate your way through and the strength of call you all have seems significant too. I thought the list of tactics from pioneers in the research was great - could you share a tactic or two you've learned?

T: A lot of what I did in the first year was to go out to deanery synods. I would go out and talk about pioneering in terms they understood. I'd use a whole load of metaphors from the rest of life - say fourteen. I'd say who do you know who is an inventor and they'd talk about Dyson and Elon Musk, or I'd talk about people gatherers and they'd talk about the lady who set up the local shop. I'd say this is roughly what a pioneer is in the church. That seemed to really work.

Another tactic I picked up from the Chief of Staff in the West Wing who is given advice by a PA who says 'don't accept the premise of the question'. So you have to say "I don't like your question I'm going to have another one that I think you should be asking". People are often saying here are the accepted norms and I am going I don't accept the premise.

R: A tactic of mine is the medium is the message - so anything I do is an opportunity to reframe things - I am always getting out tin foil, rearranging the room. Another is using the system well, gathering good stats and measuring well and using this information clearly and consistently.

A: I look harmless as a petite woman from London. That's a tactic because I am a lot more harm than people think yet by the time they realise, it's too late! So I get to the UN on somebody's half invite, wear a nice bright red jacket, sit there with my arm up, and comment at every written and oral opportunity and then ask the question at the main plenary. I might be the only woman in the room backing FGM but FGM comes up a lot and I can get it in the STG changes and then people can say it's in the STG and can get money and national policy.

I have God and God is good and I have a good sense of God and the Holy Spirit and I wouldn't survive if it wasn't for that!

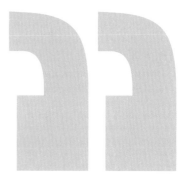

Church has a gravitational pull in on itself.
To get outside of gravity you need to get up to rocket speed"

Chris Neal

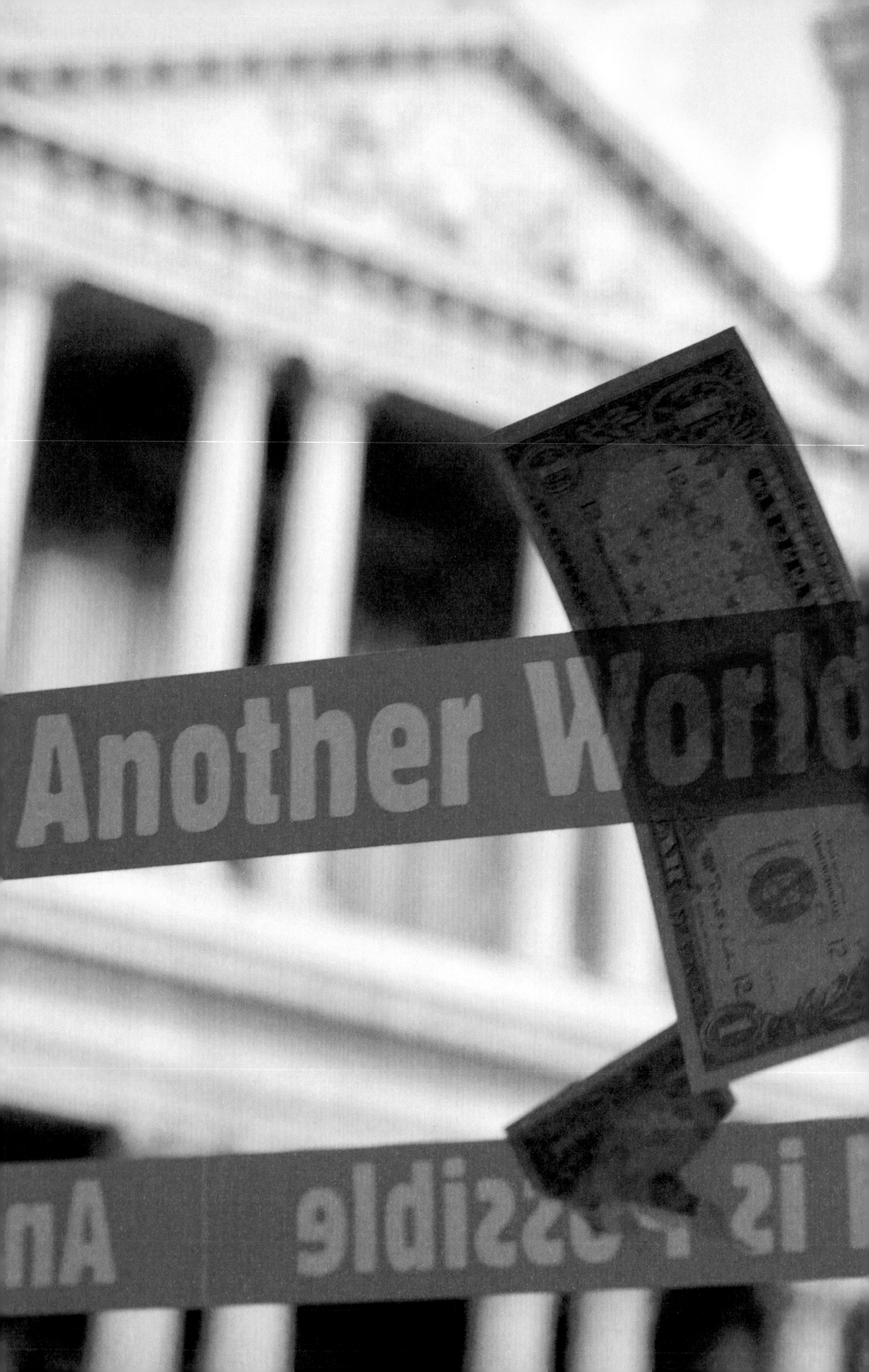
Another Worl

s Possible

Another Wo

Thinking about Change

It is really helpful to think about change and the difference your pioneering contribution makes. It can be reassuring and is good to know for yourself and team but it is also important to help others catch the vision and get behind it, and is very useful for reporting to those who have backed you. In the conversation at the start of this section, Richard and Ann-Marie both mentioned that they have theories of change and Tina described her tactics for brokering change.

Change begins with God. God's Spirit is at work in the world. In pioneering mission rather than thinking we go into a space or community to help fix it or solve something it is much more helpful to know that God is present already and at work in any space or community. Our task is one of discernment, seeing what God is doing so we can join in. And to be honest there is lots that is a complete mystery about how things happen and change – we simply have no idea other than trusting God's grace! So do hold these thoughts about change lightly within the bigger picture. But given that, these are the kind of things that might be worth thinking about:

What stories you love to tell
Your distinctive contribution
Your 'why?'
The difference it makes

Your longings
A guiding story or a metaphor

Telling stories
A great start point is noticing stories of change. Pick some of the stories you find you always love to tell that relate to your pioneering. If you are starting out look to some stories that are what have inspired you. Pioneering is all about stories in the end. Take some time to reflect on what change happens which is presumably why you love those particular stories. What happens in those stories that you think is key to that change? What was your contribution to that? Looking at stories is a great way to see the difference you make. I have done this for CMS as a whole and one of the things I noticed was that stories of pioneering I love are where someone who is an insider to a culture becomes a disciple and they then share and lead and pioneer in their own culture in imaginative ways that are authentic rather than feeling alien. That seems to be the point at which real change launches into a new phase.

Your distinctive contribution
We have included a dozen or so stories throughout this book of pioneers who have trained with us. We can't take credit for what they have done. But when I reflect on them I notice how brilliant pioneers are because they are making a difference in the world

"Lots of theories of change begin with a problem or need."

through what they see so it reminds me how important a gift that is. One of our contributions I think is simply to affirm it and say that we see, love and celebrate that gift and to advocate for it. Then I also notice how our pioneer training has sparked their imagination, encouraged them, given them some tools and language for what they are doing so the training is another contribution. And I also see that they have been hugely helped by being with other pioneers so the community of pioneers is another contribution. When it comes to thinking what is particularly distinctive that can be harder. I think taking pioneer training at CMS as an example what is distinctive compared with other training courses and colleges is that we are held within Church Mission Society which is a community that is all about pioneering across cultures so there is a real wisdom and home for what we are doing that is quite unique.

Why?

This is sometimes the hardest question to answer but finding your why is really worth some effort. Simon Sinek who has written and done TED talks on this says that it's easier to focus on and communicate what you do or how you do it. But it's much more critical and powerful to be able to share your why. Can you distil it into one short sentence?

What difference does it make?

There are lots of things for which we don't have any idea what difference we make – a seed that was planted may bear fruit much later. And the risk is that when you name those things that you can see you don't give enough attention to the hidden things like being present. But within what you do there are probably things that you can see and are differences you want to make. It can be quite easy to produce some fluffy answers that are vague and broad but can you focus it down? One tendency in church circles is to solely focus on church outcomes. I liked the conversation with Ben Thorpe because yes, one difference he wanted to make was to grow a church where there wasn't one but he also wanted to build community in that estate to make it a better world. In other words the church does not just exist for its own sake but to make a difference in the world. Measurement is looked at in the next section.

What are you longing for?

Lots of theories of change begin with a problem or need. And that can work really well. Ann-Marie is a good example of wanting to eradicate FGM in Africa which is a problem to solve. However, a deficit model isn't always helpful for mission or pioneering though it is helpful for fundraising!

▶

That's why I like the ABCD framework above whose start point is around assets in a community. One way I have found that dodges the needs approach while still giving space to what is valuable in it is to use language of longings. Then the question becomes 'what are you longing for?' rather than 'what's the problem?' So in the case of FGM we long for a world in which FGM is eradicated. It flips the emphasis somewhat.

A guiding story

Is there a guiding story or metaphor you can use to summarise what it is you are about? All the things above are helpful but a story can get to the heart of the matter simply and quickly, be evocative and draw people in. Perhaps it's a personality thing – some people respond to clear answers and statistics, others respond to something more artful. Tina is an example of using metaphor. In the conversation above she talks about how metaphor creates an alternative reality – the pioneering in Bath and Wells is called the Holy Rumpus. In terms of guiding story Safe Space in Telford use the story of Brendan the Navigator who set sail off the coast of Ireland trusting the wind of the Spirit to blow him in mission on the wild seas. They then ask where God is calling them to set sail. Many religious communities have a founding story of a Saint. At CMS we have used a gospel story with a metaphor to help refound CMS. That story is where Jesus says to the disciples 'let's go to the other side of the lake' after he has been with a crowd and they travel through a storm to Gerasa where there is a demon-possessed man in the tombs who Jesus heals. He doesn't let him come back across the lake with the disciples but sends him go to his own people as the first apostle to the Gentiles to share what God has done for him. That part of the story very much relates to the idea that the best person to share the gospel is someone inside their own culture. Jesus did minister in synagogues, in homes and with crowds but CMS' thing is always the call to the other side of the lake, the edges, beyond what is familiar, known and comfortable. Is there a metaphor or story you are drawn to for your pioneering? It might take time to explore and emerge. It's not essential but it can be powerful.

"...a story can get to the heart of the matter simply and quickly, be evocative and draw people in."

"There is fear that it will show the project isn't working well."

Measurement can be viewed a lot of different ways: dull as ditchwater, just for the form fillers, hard but necessary, or even strategic and sexy. How do you view it?

I have seen pioneers rebel against the idea of measurement. I used to be one of them. Often people don't want to focus energy on it because of one of the following reasons:

• **It takes too much time and doesn't actually tell you anything.**

• **There is fear that it will show the project isn't working well.**

• **They don't want to be judged by what someone else has deemed important.**

• **They don't believe it is really possible to measure the good that is going on in a given project, because deep down they believe it is intangible Measurement doesn't really matter.**

However, measurement does matter and it really starts with language. it begins when you get clear about the change you want to see in the world and can articulate it. When you can begin to get clear on what you want to accomplish, then you are half way to measuring it. Another way to frame the question is: What does good look like for your project?

The church often measures church attendance, money given, and sometimes volunteer hours contributed. These things came to be important because somebody thought that was evidence of something – perhaps discipleship? In some context, coming to church and giving time and money is a sign that you are growing in your faith. But it doesn't really tell us anything about the spiritual life of people coming to church. However, if you measure these things, these things become the things that matter. Or put another way, if you don't measure what matters, what you measure becomes what matters. If attendance and donations are what a church prioritizes then they will spend the majority of their time and resources creating something that people will come to and give to.

However, if that church wanted to measure the health of a Christian community, they would begin

Measuring Up

Shannon Hopkins

by articulating what a healthy Christian community looked like and then ask questions related to the current health of the community.

For pioneers there is the great opportunity to define what good looks like for their project. Figure that out, measure that, and measurement will become an asset in your work. If mission is one side of the coin, measurement is the other, and good measurement will help you stay true to your mission.

Measurement done well will:

• **Help you stay on track and avoid mission drift.**

• **Help you communicate the impact you are making.**

• **Help you win over new stakeholders**

• **Give you confidence about what is really working and what isn't.**

• **Help you make better decisions.**

Measurement helps you know more than you knew before and for that reason it can help you make better decisions. After all, don't you want to know if what you are doing is working?

There are two easy ways to start measuring:

1. Talk to people. Measurement can begin by simply gathering information from the people you are working with.

2. Run a confidence test.

Here is an example of a confidence test. If you run a project to help X happen:

1. Define X. For example: "I want to help people be less anxious."

2. Ask your team: How confident are we that people in our program are less anxious?

3. Ask your team: What makes you so confident people are less anxious? LIisten to the stories... what is the evidence telling you?
When you answer those two questions together you have some evidence!

We need to make sure the measuring stick we are using for our projects is actually helping us learn and improve.

Don't fear measurement. Use it to find out you are doing and as a tool to help you achieve your desired impact.

This reflection is pitched at those supervising pioneers. So if you are a pioneer pass this on or use this as the basis of a discussion if you have someone in the structures supporting or supervising you.

Supervision & Support

Tina Hodgett

Autonomy is important because pioneers are often activists who work on the basis of dream, intuition and hypothesis. They need space from 'things as they are' in order to think, and thrive on freedom from enclosing structures. They are self-starters who prefer to make mistakes and learn from them rather than follow well-trodden paths and stay safe in a known world that could be changed by trying a few things out. This does mean for the supervisor you are more likely to have to pick up the pieces if the pioneer makes a mistake than you are to prevent the mistake from happening in the first place. This can be an uncomfortable place to be, but if the pioneer feels trusted she/he is more likely to ask for advice and support when thin ice appears. It is also why it's important to offer access.

Access to decision-makers is important for pioneers within an existing system. When they sense their instincts may be too disruptive of the existing order or threaten relationship, or that they may be taking too great a risk for the supervisor and institution to manage, they want to touch base with authority figures for a steer. Access balances autonomy - a pioneer can work a long way from their supervising structures, but use a hotline for those occasions when decisions need to be made at a higher level of authority, or where reassurance is needed.

Advocacy Even though pioneer mission may attract attention or be seen as 'sexy', the vast majority of all the church's resources are still directed towards inherited church, and church legal and organisational structures uphold the status quo. Pioneers need supervisors to be advocates for them and their work at the next level of responsibility. Like other minorities, they need to have role models, and feel 'seen' and understood. If they have to expend energy on advocating for themselves in the church it will reduce the energy and attention they will be able to give in mission. Without these three gifts a pioneer may not survive in post.

The gift of autonomy is not an excuse to do whatever the pioneer likes. The relationship with the supervisor and others in the structure is really important. It always goes best when that relationship is genuinely founded on mutual trust and respect which takes time, good listening and understanding of one another. It tends to go wrong when there is suspicion and a lack of trust especially if that manifests itself as tighter control which can really stifle a pioneer. Most pioneers appreciate the need for good connection and will have high expectations of themselves, while wanting to avoid questions about quantitative outcomes of their work because of the risk that such outcomes drive decision-making and prevent missioners from following the lead of the Holy Spirit. It can be difficult for others to understand this apparent paradox. Pioneers appreciate good questions, and may occasionally need to be helped to listen to themselves when they are in dreaming mode and allowing enthusiasm to outrun wisdom.

A formula for enabling a pioneer to flourish:

Autonomy + Access + Advocacy X an environment of mutual trust

= a flourishing pioneer and great possibility

The development of an environment of mutual trust can be helped by the pioneer through things like:

• **a commitment to be in good relationship with the supervisor and the wider structures as far as it is in her/his power**

• **good communication**

• **willingness to accept the wisdom and authority of the supervisor, particularly in respect of the relationship with wider structures**

• **an understanding that spiritual discernment belongs to the whole church**

• **professional standards as contextually appropriate**

• **commitment to safeguarding principles and practice**

• **commitment to risk management and matters of health and safety**

• **willingness to play a part in resourcing the work if appropriate**

The development of an environment of mutual trust can be helped by the supervisor through things like:

• **a commitment to take the time to understand the pioneer and their work and to be for them**

• **good communication**

• **not being controlling or parental**

• **showing genuine interest outside of formal meetings**

• **advocating for the pioneer**

Mutual trust between pioneer and their supervisor enables an environment which allows new things to emerge. It creates a secure space for the pioneer to play, and as such would be useful for all those with responsibility for the flourishing of pioneers to further the associated awareness, practice and skills needed to provide this kind of space as widely as possible for the emergence of a God-inspired newness.

Support
Part of building trust will be ensuring the pioneer has effective support. I haven't included 'support' in the formula, but it is crucial. Pioneering can be a lonely and challenging path to tread, even with a local team and a good supervisor. Discuss with your pioneer what kind of support they hope to have. Often they will have their own networks, but a local network will be useful. Each pioneer will have their own ideas about what constitutes support – it might be the opportunity to offload, it might be a family to belong to, spiritual direction, a small prayer group, supervisor and/or congregation members showing an interest in how the work is progressing, it might be signposting to other places where pioneering stuff is happening. Find out rather than assume what will be helpful and make a point of negotiating this on a regular basis as circumstances change.

How To Lead When Things Are

Shannon Hopkins

Often something will happen in your context, internally or externally, that impacts your work and demands that you adjust. This can be disruptive, but that doesn't necessarily mean it is a bad thing. It can provide the impetus to pivot. When things are disrupted something new can break in. Disruption can equal opportunity, allowing you to take risks and make changes that you wouldn't otherwise have made.

After training entrepreneurs to tackle wicked problems and think in new ways, the organization I founded, Matryoshka House, found itself in a place where the model we were operating from was no longer working. We had to do what we have advised others: we had to pivot.

From this experience, we have identified five distinct phases of a pivot, five stages to go through when the structures you've built no longer work.

Stage 1 Recognition

Recognition opens the door for change but our human nature often resists change. Recognition is often the hardest stage in the pivoting process. You have to see that something isn't working. Our cognitive bias tends to retell a narrative in a way that suggests something is working or that the lessons or outcome achieved made it all worth it. To recognize that something isn't working does not mean that nothing good has come from the work, rather that the 'good' does not fully reflect the intended impact.

Stage 2 Grief

"No one ever told me that grief felt so like fear."
C.S. Lewis, A Grief Observed

Once you recognize that things have to change, that things can't go on as they are, there is a loss that is experienced, and along with that, a deep fear because of the uncertainty of what will replace it. Grief is a necessary response to loss and it plays a role in moving us through the change process. Christians are a people that believe in a gospel of death and resurrection. But too often we rush from death to resurrection and we don't acknowledge the pain and the loss. The challenge here is to not rush or move on too quickly. You need to actually acknowledge the loss and make space for the feelings.

Sometimes, the grief was as much about the lost ideal as anything else. It is important in this step to recognize and acknowledge what we are losing, and we need to feel our feelings. If you cannot acknowledge what is being lost it is impossible to move forward into the future with health.

Grief by necessity needs a way to commemorate and memorialise. At MH, we created a ritual to allow ourselves, our community, and other stakeholders the space to mourn and celebrate. Our "ritual" was a service that allowed other people to mark the changes with us, celebrate the past and pray for the future.

Falling Apart

Stage 3 Learning

You don't want to sit in grief forever. You need to find a way to sift through the rubble and pull out the essential and meaningful parts from the past, but you also need to identify the assumptions that were problematic. Here in this step we start to see the things we want to take with us into the future and the things that we need to leave behind.

One of the best things that happens at funerals is the stories that get told and the memories that get shared. Learning happens best when you make space for deep listening to multiple groups of people.

One of the most beautiful and powerful things that happened at our ritual was the people who came back from across the various seasons to talk about how they had been impacted and how the ripples were going out. Our work was having a lasting impact, still shaping peoples' families, community, and work in different places and in more powerful ways than we knew. There was gold in that, and whatever we do next, we want to create more ripple effects!

Stage 4 Renewed Vision

He who has a why can endure any how.'
Frederick Nietzsche

There has been a lot of talk in recent years about "knowing your why." In step four you must grab hold of your why. Your why is what helps you get back in the ring. When you truly grab hold of your why again, then the how you do your work and the what you do doesn't matter. What matters is the end to which you are working. What is your desired impact? What transformation will you see in people, places, policy and/or systems if you are successful? When you think through the lens of impact and purpose, then you can more easily redesign the how and the what. This is the step where hope can break back in.

Stage 5 Reimagined Practice

"Live out of your imagination, not your history."
Steven R. Covey

Once you get clearer on your why and the impact you want to have, then you can reimagine the how. This is where new practice can be developed. In stage five, we hit the place where it is time to be brave again. But as you start again, you start with eyes wide open. Knowing more than you knew before, you get back in the ring.

Charles Handy wrote in The Second Curve: "Anything that takes us out of our comfort zones for a while can act as a reminder that the past we are used to may not be our best future"

For us, our pivot ended with a birth of new things. We decided to spin out all of our work into three new organizations, two in the UK and one in the US, and to the let the community be a self-organizing community. Rather than holding onto the complexity we once cherished before, it allows each organization to focus on its mission and landscape and live out its prophetic imagination.

So, when you are faced with needing things to change, lean into the discomfort and pivot! Let it be a season to start again from a new place. It most likely will lead you to a better future!

THE
POW
THAT BE

There is a confusing paradox in many organisations and churches. They know they need to change so are aware that pioneers bring a much needed and important gift. After all if any organisation gets stuck and doesn't change it will die. So it is common for pioneers to pick up and hear that the gift they bring is wanted and to feel excited about that. And yet the very same organisations and churches are simultaneously resistant to change, to newness, and at times directly opposed to it. This opposition can be utterly baffling and make pioneers wonder what they have done. I have seen it make people ill because of the level of toxicity. I have worked now for over a decade training, supporting, encouraging and helping pioneers in multiple contexts. I am honestly not exaggerating. In the survey pioneers said the top thing most likely to derail pioneering is the powers that be so you know this is real.

It is to do with culture - people are used to things being a certain way and like it. So change is a threat. Culture is very powerful and will eat strategies for breakfast! FGM is a huge part of some African cultures so Ann-Marie Wilson (see Change conversation) has to pay attention to culture in order to bring change.

It is to do with expectations. The kind of pioneering needed certainly in the church is creative ways of thinking about church that are as close as possible to people who are culturally a long way from the way we do church and that means there will be very different expressions and theology, much of which

may be unrecognisable to those at the centre. Meanwhile on the church end pioneering is most easily understood the more like the existing church the new thing looks - a building, Sundays, a priest, singing, preaching and money going to the diocese for example - and that can be the expectation which may not have been explicitly named. A clash of expectations is very common.

It is to do with visibility. A pioneer can be working outside the walls of the church, building community connections and relationships and seeing all sorts of wonderful things happening. Yet others look and they simply don't seem to see what's going on. To the pioneer it's obvious and to the organization, it's hidden or invisible.

It is to do with people. Sometimes pioneers can be their own worst enemy if they are challenging and difficult and don't do the relational work or act from love or kindness. Equally it is not uncommon to find there are one or two people in the structures who work to undermine pioneering sometimes overtly, sometimes in hidden ways and sometimes in horrid ways.

It is to do with power or perhaps powers. Pioneers generally go to the edge, to the margins and don't have a lot of resource or power and I think that's a good thing. It's the way of Christ. Our struggle is not against people, it's against the powers. The powers can be against you and at times it feels like that is a deeper power than simply the people

holding office. There isn't space here to explore a theology of the powers though that is a fascinating area. I like Walter Wink's exploration where he suggests institutions have a spirit, angel or personality, a life of their own. It feels like that. I am of the view that Jesus was killed because of his resistance to the powers of empire and religious domination. As the pioneer of our faith he saw and proposed an alternative way and the powers didn't like it one bit. It's not rational. It's why prayer and acting in the opposite spirit to the powers is so important. In my conversation above with Ann-Marie, Tina, Richard who are involved in system or culture change it was clear they are dealing with powers in this way.

This all sounds pretty terrifying frankly. Why get involved?! The answer to that is you can't help it because it's who you are! But it's worth naming I think so that you expect it and are prepared and consider that the work in the direction of the sponsoring organisation or church is an important part of the overall pioneering.

The summary above from answers to the survey question 'What tactics have you learned about change within wider structures or systems' is full of practical wisdom on this. I loved pulling that together. I would print it off and stick it on your wall or put it in your wallet as a reminder. I will just highlight or re-emphasise a few of those insights

In terms of change you need to create new practice on the ground. Unless people can see it they won't get it. So a priority should be making stuff happen rather than simply talking about it. And then communicate it in language that the institution understands. Apply the cross-cultural skills you use with those at the edges to those at the centre.

Then secondly system change requires not just dissent or pioneering that leads to new practice on the ground. It also requires authority dissent. By that I mean someone in the structures who is able to broker the space for the pioneering and advocate for it in committees and boards, to root for you, to cover your back and so on. It's tempting to think pioneering dissent is enough on its own but deep change is very difficult to achieve without that combination so who do you know that can be that sponsor for you in your pioneering? Give time and effort to that relationship.

Then don't assume you are on the same page as the organisation. They may not know what you are doing or imagining. So write stuff down, talk it through, get it agreed and minuted. Again talk their language.

And lastly be nice, show up on time, be kind, listen, give time to the relationships at that end as well as the ones at the edges. Of course be true, but be someone who is likeable and easy to work with as far as you possibly can. The relational stuff makes so much difference.

And sometimes all you can do is pray.

ROAD CLOSED

"...sometimes all you can do is

PR

AY."

"The act of praying itself is one of the indispensable means by which we engage the powers. It is in fact that engagement at its most fundamental level, where their secret spell over us is broken and we are re-established in a bit more of that freedom which is our birthright and potential."

Walter Wink

Movements
Change The World

Andrea Campanale

Human-built structures tend to be fixed, static and have definite limitations in terms of how much they move or can be modified. Think of buildings, furniture and even vehicles. Robust and solid makes us feel safe and in control. Contrast that with nature. Water, trees and our own physical bodies are created to move, to change and to grow. This is a normal sign of healthy development. There is form and a certain degree of predictability, but also plenty of room for flow, resistance and mess. This is why I love networks. They too generate life, energy and the limitless potential for creativity, diversity and new possibility. To overly manage is to risk their death.

Movements change the world. Whether it's the abolition of slavery, the end of communism in Eastern Europe or Extinction Rebellion. In church history, movements have brought about a necessary corrective to complacency that creeps into institutional structures. Francis of Assisi challenged the wealth of the Roman Catholic Church in the 13th century and the charismatic renewal movement of the 1970s made space for a fresh wave of the Spirit of God. When I started doing outreach to spiritual seekers in 2005, I honestly thought I was alone in wanting to bring the message of the love of Christ to a different people group in new and creative ways. It gave me such hope and encouragement to discover through CMS others grappling with the same questions and challenges that I was experiencing. There was

a language of pioneering and fresh expressions of church to describe what I was seeking to do. And I began to see that I was part of a wider move of the Holy Spirit that could not only renew the church, but might also change the world! Well my bit of it anyway.

Earlier in the year, I read Alastair McIntosh's book 'Soil and Soul' and was greatly inspired by his take on activism. I don't think McIntosh would describe himself as a Christian, yet he draws on the biblical narrative and a Celtic Christian heritage which is rooted in our British isles and culture. His view is that if you are engaged in community development or environmental activism you are not just taking on the forces of capitalism or secularism, but are engaging the 'Powers'. This comes from the idea that behind corporations and institutions are spiritual entities which conflict with the priorities and values of the Kingdom of God. McIntosh, therefore, suggests campaigners should be both fuelled and resourced spiritually, and be part of a community or network of like-minded individuals. This will ensure they're not isolated and will keep them from giving in to despair. In his words, "Maybe the 'prophetic' task for our times is to find the remnant community of activists who care - the bleeding hearts and artists; the scientists and the practical people - and to

▶

gather ourselves into movements. Maybe the name of the game is to identify remnant islands of both human culture and natural ecology, and to nurture them: to help them find the angelic manna that will rebuild their strength, even for those on the verge of death."

As someone who has found pioneering to be wonderfully exciting and energising, but also profoundly disappointing and frustrating, I really resonate with this sentiment. The research with pioneers shows how difficult it can be at times. The top answer to what pioneers wish they knew when they started out is how hard it is with church structures and systems. The top answer to the question of what is most likely to derail pioneering is resistance from the powers that be. Our experience which is also borne out by wider research is that it is invaluable if not essential for pioneers to be in a network or community that gets pioneering. It can offer like-mindedness, friendship, support, and be a space where you don't have to explain yourself. So do connect with others into some sort of network or group around pioneering.

The Starfish Network
The Starfish Network is the CMS pioneer network of those who have done at least one module of training. Over a decade the pioneer training has grown and developed to encompass a variety of training pathways that include ordinands as well as lay people, youth and children's workers and entrepreneurs. There are now a number of hubs and centres. I and the team of representatives of current and former students from the Pioneer Mission Leadership Training, have been dreaming and reflecting together on how we can better nurture Starfish as a 'remnant island' helping one another to find 'angelic manna' such that we will stay fit and resilient as pioneers active in seeking to extend God's Kingdom. By way of example of how a movement that is networked grows I outline below how we have developed that and are nurturing it ten years on.

At the heart of the network is a shared commitment and passion for pioneering mission. That is what we're about and sums up our distinctive. Our values are imagination, participation, freedom and risk and we seek to embody these in our pioneering practice and in the training. We see community, prayer and learning as ways to fuel pioneering mission. We have tried to write these down as simply as we can as our 'True North' – see below.

We've identified what we're aiming to provide in Starfish as GARB: Gathering; Affirming; Resourcing; and Belonging. The gathering we do at events through the year such as conversations days, a Fiesta and hosting meet ups at Greenbelt and elsewhere. The resourcing happens as we share on our Facebook page and in an online forum, as well as Starfish members teaching and facilitating modules in the pioneer hubs. We want to create a new gathering where we affirm each other in the ministry of pioneering whether someone has been officially recognised as a pioneer or not, and we've begun to see Starfish regional groups hosted by hubs creating on-going communities of pioneering practice and learning for our members at a local or regional level.

Another idea we've been exploring is creating a light touch rhythm of life. This could incorporate spiritual practices and include a specially written community prayer and other prayers, practices, rituals and liturgy created by pioneers to draw from. As outlined in the True North section on prayer there is no set prayer book – we're not that kind of community but do want to creatively nourish our faith together.

Like A Murmaration
We need multiple networks and communities that nurture and affirm pioneers in their unique gift and ministry. Starfish is just one. We need to connect to one another to be part of the wider movement. We need to continue to find our hope and strength in our Christian faith as we improvise out of the tradition to build one another up. This is so we might not just enable greater maturity in Christ as individuals, but that this movement we're forming and growing, like a murmuration of starlings, will indeed impact the world such that it becomes more like the heaven on earth Jesus encouraged us to pray for.

"Despite all the struggles, pioneering as a vocation is not easy to get out from under. The call of the wild, it draws you to the uninhabited spaces, to follow dreams that are too ridiculous to be expressed, to build places you've only seen in your imagination. And no matter how beat up you are, how hacked off or desperate for rest, when the call of the Spirit comes again you're up and throwing a few things into a bag and off again, probably limping, sniffing the air, catching the scent."

Kim Brown

What Have We Learned? →

A conversation about pioneering

Paul Bradbury set up Poole Missional Communities and Reconnect which has been both a community of around 40-50 people and a charity which has been an umbrella for a range of pioneering initiatives.

Andrea Campanale has pioneered mission with spiritual seekers at mind body spirit fairs and set up a mission community in Kingston.

Kim Brown set up the Upper Room in Cirencester – her story is above.

They have all been part of the pioneering adventure for some time so I caught up with them to glean some of their wisdom and reflections.

J: In the research above people describe pioneering in five ways - finding a new path, seeing possibilities, building stuff, responding to injustice, starting new forms of church where church isn't. I really liked that and thought it was about right. What's your sense?

K: Responding to injustice and growing a new form of church where church wasn't were our two. The injustice was twofold - that some people weren't welcomed in church as well as the wider injustices in society that affected them. We were left with no choice - it was a burning inside keeping me awake at night like a vibration in my body that I had to do something about. I couldn't get away from it - but it took a damn long time to get it done.

A: It's always been about the disconnect between where ordinary people are and the church. And feeling that there was something in the gospel that was applicable to these people that they were never going to get because of the chasm that existed between the world and the church. That was always my starting point. And then it developed into a realisation that the evangelism going on was aimed at people who were well off and didn't really feel like they needed God. And yet there was this other stuff going on with people who were seeking so it was a no brainer to connect with those who were actually interested. It was seeing that possibility, seeing that potential to do something creative and new with a people group who were never going to be attracted to what existed already. Different people have different start points - for some it's church; for others it's an engagement with the world.

P: When I started I thought it was all about others who needed to hear the gospel and not about the institution. I didn't feel invested in the institution. But more recently I think I realise that pioneers are passionate about the church, about God's people, that community that holds the life and witness of Jesus in a place. More and more I see pioneers sitting in that difficult space between the tradition and those that are a long way away from it, who feel

like they are never going to connect with it. How do we bridge that gap in a way that's authentic to the tradition and that community? I used to think that tradition was a bit moribund but I have wanted to reclaim it as a really good thing and pioneers can be positive about it through a creative improvisation of what tradition means in this new place among this new people.

J: Pioneering is nothing new. If you take a dictionary of saints the church celebrates they are almost all pioneers. But the language around pioneer surfaced in the current iteration off the back of the church report Mission Shaped Church in 2004 as a way of saying that people starting new things bring a different gift or approach and the church to its credit named it and said it wanted to encourage it. What are your reflections looking back?

K: In terms of my own experience it was mixed. We were simply a group of women from different churches who were desperate to respond to people we met who were desperate. We didn't know anything. The church we were in did not welcome this and some of us had to leave. Then the C of E picked us up. I felt a call to ordination and then got a job working in a charismatic church and they trained me up a bit. As I was going through training the report you mention had come out (Mission Shaped Church) and trickled to Gloucester which is very rural and not always fastest getting into new things. But then our Bishop, Michael Perham, went on a tour of fresh expressions and looked at lots of pioneer settings. He was pretty open minded. He said I should get ordained and gave us a BMO (Bishops' Mission Order - this is a piece of legislation such that a fresh expression that is not a parish can fit as an entity within the Church of England' structures). So we became a permanent part of the structure here and that gave us room to breathe but never any money other than via the curacy. As soon as my curacy finished there was no money - I was really broke for a while. It was a pretty grim. There is a sense that the church wants pioneering, they

like it and it's all 'Yes yes! On you go!' but at times there's nothing behind that to back it up and support the new life. I am skeptical about the church's commitment to it really.

A: I am still waiting for a BMO and it's taken about five years to get to this point. So it's long and slow and has taken a lot of persistence and perseverance.

J: The research we did shows that the challenges people face are very real in relation to navigating the structures, and overcoming resistance.

P: It does come down to personalities too. We had an archdeacon who was entrepreneurial and he persuaded the diocese to fund some pioneer posts. We have kept going despite not getting a lot of funding. The BMO also helped because it created some space within which to operate. Every diocese is its own fiefdom and it's patchy.

K: The church is much bigger than that which self-identifies as being the church. Once you get out you see church all over the place and people connected with God in all kinds of other ways. There have been lots of movements down the ages that have resonated and captured people's imaginations such as Celtic spirituality or 24/7 prayer. There are people out there that know more than the institution. Pioneering has broadened the experience of the church more I think.

J: What would you say to people starting out knowing what you know now?

P: Don't do it!

K: You're going to work hard, not get a lot of sleep and be broke for the next ten years but go for it! (roars of laughter all round). It's the worst thing and the best thing all rolled into one. It costs but it mustn't put you off. If there is something burning in you you need to let it burn into a flame and do something with that energy and power that it pro-

pels you with as you try and sleep at night and ignore it because it isn't going to go away until you've done it. It's like being pregnant - it's a very weird long pregnancy and you have to accept it and give birth to it even though it's painful - but it will be brilliant.

A: It's also fun. There's nothing as fulfilling or exhilarating or purposeful as when things are coming together and the idea is exciting and new and people start coming to it and things start to move and you see the positive fruits of it - there's just nothing better. But it's not always like that! There are cycles - maybe it's like the grief cycle. There's a buzz, you consolidate, it starts to wane, and you need a new impetus new imagination new people coming with something to kickstart it again.

P: You are going to learn as much about yourself as pioneering. It's taken me on a huge personal journey. When I started at 36 straight out of curacy you think you've got the answers and are doing something cool and whizzy and entrepreneurial and the church looks to you even though it's not going to give you much money. It looks to you for some of the answers to its woes and you find yourself in a situation where you carry a lot of hope for the church. I got to the point after five years where things weren't working out and almost had a breakdown and a kind of conversion. I went through a real death and resurrection experience which was really about whose ministry it is. Is it me and my abilities or God and his Holy Spirit? I learned that personally. Leaders in mission follow that call to place ourselves in real vulnerability where there's nothing else that can take place unless God shows up - that's what you learn! There's something about the comfort of the established church that can protect you from that - not always but a lot of the time it does. I'd say be prepared to go through a fairly harrowing personal journey but coming out much healthier the other side because you have learned something about the leadership of the Holy Spirit.

A: I think I wasted lot of time trying to explain and

get everybody on side. It took a lot of energy. It was better when I got on and did it., Then people could see it and say oh that's what you meant. Don't look for that approval or permission - just do it. Go for it, step out, try stuff.

K: I guess looking back I didn't have a big picture at the outset; I just lurched along and felt like I was in the dark. I began to become comfortable with not knowing, trundling along and then there being moments of epiphany. It's God's thing - you are a custodian, a surrogate, pregnant with it, but it doesn't belong to you. You are just a holder, a partner and you learn to cooperate with the Holy Spirit over time and to get out of the way of it and let it happen. It isn't yours. I always felt I was a person being invited along for the ride, the impetus wasn't me, it was external to me. The other thing you discover is that the Missio Dei is for real. Everywhere you look when you get out of the old building God is just at work everywhere. Even in a really cursory glance you just see God at work. I shouldn't have been but was surprised how in the homeless community I found God. Guys on the street taught me masses about God. You learn to trust in the madness of it all after a while. You know you are going to find him wherever you go. I got to a mid-point a few years in and then simply let the chaos unfold and relaxed without trying to control it.

J: What's helped keep you going?

P: It's forced me to be disciplined about a quiet day a month, regular rhythms of retreat and prayer and reflection and reading. I couldn't have survived if I didn't score out a day a month, a retreat each year and that sort of thing to recentre myself and stop myself trying to rush things and get ahead of what God is doing and keep in tune with the pace of the Spirit. And I think the other thing is good theology in the sense that pioneering continues to be contested - other people writing to give a basis for what we were doing was helpful especially when I got despondent. I'd go 'this is theologically well rooted' and that gave me impetus to keep going because it wasn't just a pipe dream but was rooted in some good missional theology.

A: The relationships with people in the community, having a support structure, spreading the risk so I don't just get income from one source, but have a few different things going on. If you are reliant on one institution to be your support then if there's a problem you are set adrift. I have a counsellor, a spiritual director, a mentor - I take all the help I can get! That keeps me from falling off the edge.

K: Learn to build your self disciplines and support structures because it is lonely. You're gestating something and you can't necessarily say what it is. You have a lot of opposition and sometimes there's not a lot to show for all the angst, so you do need other people around to help lift you up and drag you along on the rotten days. When I came to start to train at CMS I started to go to a monastery once a month for spiritual direction and a quiet day. I still see my spiritual director there and he's connected to a few other pioneer groups so he is a wise head who makes me stop, get some perspective and have a laugh when I am ranting and raving about what's happening. The high you get from seeing stuff actually happening when you see people begin to grasp it and take their own journey forward and have those kind of moments of God for themselves – when things shift in their lives – you feel the huge joy of having been a teeny part of that and it's rewarding in itself. That's what keeps me getting out of bed in the morning, knowing that I could absolutely rely on God to show up in whatever way God decided. You'd know some stuff was going to happen every time you went outside.

J: Where does pioneering go next?

P: The sense I get is that on the ground there is a real hunger for the wisdom and experience that pioneers offer - people recognise post-Covid that they have got to do something different. It's been accelerated or multiplied on the ground. The future will be much more ground up than top down. It won't be driven by diocesan policy but by pioneers and vicars on the ground going we've got to work together and innovate.

K: The next phase I see is more financial struggles in the institutional church, so paid posts will be even harder to find. Maybe we'll go back to more seed-corn, grassroots work; people just doing stuff and the institution won't be in a position to fight with it. It could continue to be hard financially - there will be a lot more tent making. It some ways that spreads the load because more people have to get involved.

A: I have talked to younger pioneers and they say they haven't had to fight. They have been recognised, had training, feel supported, and are able to do what God has called them to do which is great. So I think for some people things have shifted and they look at me and say 'that's your experience but it's not been ours'. We need to find creative ways to mobilise and encourage one another. We have those means, those mechanisms so now is the time to start using them.

True North ⬆

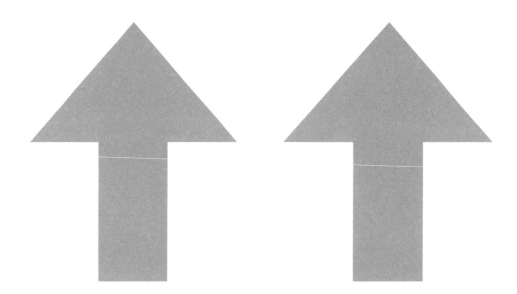

True North orients or pulls in a particular direction. That direction is God's mission. True North is a metaphor for what is at the heart of the pioneer gift as we have reflected on it over ten years. The CMS pioneer network, Starfish (see above) orients around this. We seek to align our lives with God's mission, to participate in it and to support one another in doing so. But it probably describes the pioneer gift for many whether in that network or not.

What we are about:
Pioneering Mission

What gets us out of bed in the morning is pioneering mission. This can be opened up in many ways. But it is a call into the world beyond the edges of the church, beyond business as usual, to share good news and join in with creation's healing, with what God is doing. Pioneering is a gift of seeing, of imagination, of dreaming. And it is a gift of building, doing, making things happen in response.

While the whole world needs to hear the gospel pioneers gravitate particularly to the edges.

The edges where people and creation herself are broken, poor, weak, vulnerable, lost. Why? It seems like Jesus did so and we seek to follow him. We seek to be, live and model a life on Christ who is our best pattern and example, and to pioneer in the spirit of Christ the Pioneer of our faith.

As the Father sent Jesus so Jesus sends us - into cultures, places, people, localities, across boundaries to share the gospel. The gospel is always culturally robed so the sharing requires a letting go of our own ways, a listening and discerning to discover afresh the gospel in a new culture. Do it from the inside. This is an adventure of the imagination.

What we value: Freedom, Imagination, Participation, Risk

There is great freedom in Christ. This freedom is about being yourself, about how to follow Christ, about what resources you draw on. You are unique, made in God's image. Your life's work is to become more fully who you are, to open up that gift. You are not called to be what anyone else thinks you should be or do - be you.

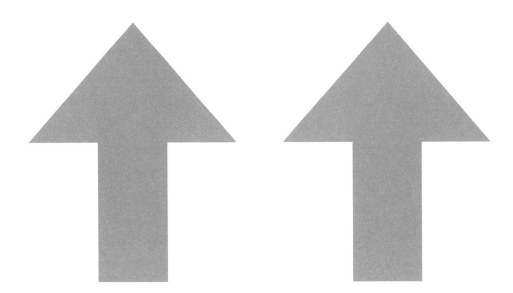

Mission is an adventure of the imagination. We are seers and dreamers, who love imagining what's possible, what we can do and not what we can't do. That imagination is about how to unfurl to heal the world, how to join in with God's mission, to participate in the world's healing.

Faith is active. So we live a life of mission in our context out of who we are called to be. That participation can be many things and will ebb and flow. But we are not passive observers of God's mission; we are dreamers who do.

Someone said that faith is spelled RISK and that makes us smile. We are up for risk, crossing boundaries, and going to places and being with people others might avoid. We try things out, experiment, play.

What fuels us: Prayer, Community, Learning

We pray. It doesn't matter how or when - there's no set prayer book. But a life of pioneering mission is fuelled by prayer. We draw on the riches of others to inspire our prayer - the world church, our own traditions, religious communities. And we write and create our own to express our particular longings. We depend on God. We grieve for what is broken. We hope for what can be.

There is a stereotype of pioneers as lone individuals but it's rarely good to simply pioneer or be alone. For us it is about team, being together. We are warmed, encouraged and supported by friendship and community with other pioneers. And in our pioneering we creatively explore and work out how to follow Christ with others in community.

We value the wisdom and learning from others - about God, about the world, about mission. We ask questions, we are curious and hungry to explore. We don't seek ready made answers off the shelf but reflect on our own experience drawing on this wisdom. We immerse ourselves in the scriptures to better understand and live our lives in the way of Christ. We learn through reading, through conversation, through study, through doing, through community, through others.

CMS
Website - pioneer.churchmissionsociety.org
Twitter - @CMSpioneer

Why train with CMS?

Be understood.

A course by pioneers for pioneers. We get it and we will help you help others get it. Our students discover a language that works.

Be recognised.

The pioneering gift should be recognised and appreciated. Our qualifications are accredited by Durham University.

Be trusted.

A whole 200+ year mission community and a vast network behind you who believe in you. Really.

Be supported.

You can't do this alone. You'll be part of a dynamic learning community and wider network of pioneer hubs and friends.

Be you.

Connect and learn with others like you who have discovered the freedom of not fitting in.

GETsidetracked.co

info@getsidetracked.co

Jonny Baker
Blog - jonnybaker.blogs.com
Instagram - @bonnyjaker
Twitter - @jonnybaker
Photos - flickr.com/photos/jonnybaker

Jon Birch
Website - www.jonbirchartist.com
Instagram - @jonbirch_artist
Facebook - @jonbirchartist

Thank you to everyone who has contributed to Pioneer Practice so generously with your time, writing and photos.

Photos in stories from story contributors
p134 & p137 photos by **Jon Birch**
all other photos by **Jonny Baker**

Design, illustration & layout **Jon Birch**

The cover image and the image on p118
are tiles made by sculptor **Iain Cotton** for all
CMS pioneers when they graduate.
A new unique journey has been hewn or painted on the stone landscape to make a way where there is no way. The path also looks like a letter or script and plays with the notion of a new language that is found in the journey.

Story tellers, conversation partners
and article writers -
David Harrigan
Adam Gompertz
Jo Howie
Miriam Wakefield
Tim Thorlby
Erika Biscoe
Kim Brown
Anna Hembury
Harvey Kwiyani
Meg Fry
Paul Bradbury
Andrea Campanale
Andy Freeman
Johnny Sertin
Michael Mitton
Sue Steer
Gavin Mart
Ben Thorpe
Shannon Hopkins
Tina Hodgett
Ann Marie Wilson
Richard Passmore

Pioneers at CMS who have trusted us to train whether in a module, a hub, or an award. You have been the ones who have made a way where there is no way with your pioneer practice. You are incredible people and a community who bring hope to the world and indeed the church.

The pioneer team at CMS over the last ten years –
Cathy Ross, Sarah Clarke, Andrea Campanale, Andy Freeman, Johnny Sertin, James Butler, Lynda Gerrard, Helen Harwood, Colin Smith, Harvey Kwiyani and all those who have lectured, mentored, shared stories and led hubs.

Friends who have been companions on the way who have shown solidarity, been advocates and given encouragement. You are too many to mention and we would risk forgetting some if we started a list, but thank you.

*Thank you to all the readers who
helped make the project happen
by kickstarting us:*

Dan Corcoran
Craig Mitchell
Sally Rush
Rob Ryan
Michael Mitton
Martyn Woodsford
Graham Potter
Jenny Bourne
Dawn Abbatt
Harry & Grace Rae
Judy
Ben & Beth Honey
Steve Atkins
Fiona Mayne
Yvonne Mullins
John Tasker
Dustin Benac
Daniel Dupree
Barney Barron
Sarah Clarke
Gavski
Holly Rankin Zaher
Heather Cracknell
Joy Wadsworth
Dr. Edward Pillar
Linda Sines
Rebecca Rock
Sue Vallente Kerr
Felix Goldinger
Rebecca W Keller
Sarah Hewitt
Sonia Mainstone-Cotton
Helen Dowdell
Jo Dolby
Bob Carlton
Joel & Kat Baker
Mike Gower
Andrew Dunlop
Sarah Cracknell
Thomas Brackett
Susan
Caroline Bishop
Sandy Brodine
Shannon Hopkins
Miriam Wakefield
Georgina Burrell
Mark Fletcher
Lindy Cameron
Katharina Haubold
David & Kathy Bland
Hannah Steele
David Hillyer
Derrick Watson
David Wynd
Hugh Stradling
Matt Davis
Aad Vermeyden
Patrick Douglas

Tim Soerens
Kevin & Lucy Read
Frances Shoesmith
Dave Salsbury
Pete Broadbent
Ben Hudd
Remco van den Heuvel
Rev Claire Alcock
Tim Watson
Martin Lawson
Janice Hamilton
Andy Weeds
Colin Smith
Kenda Dean
Martin Wroe
Chris Sheehan
Tim Thorlby
Clivison & Eli de Santana
Frauke Eicker
William Perry
Peter Hughes
Martin Groth
Catherine Patterson
Sam Tyndall
Jane Emson
Tim Yau
Ali Middleton
Oli Preston
Mollie Herron
Christopher Ramsay
Geoff Maddock
Nikky Mungeam
Paul Tester
Sue Wallace
Heath Monaghan
Gary Daniel
Jon & Tammy Oliver
Diane & Steve Eyre
Steve Price
Ian Macdonald
Tim Van Meter
Andrea MacPherson
Lucy Barbour
Kevin Colyer
Tricia Frith
Erika Biscoe
David G Palmer
Mark Inglis
Mandy Dunstall
Howard Dunn
Debbie Budge
Revd. Alan Moss
Deborah Pardoe
Andy Jefferson
Kiri
Jo Howie
Sandra Bils
Margaret Fisher

Andy Lindley
David Muir
Pauline Randall
Ros Wakefield
Tim Lea
Belinda Ngugi
Chandra Morbey
Daniel Gentner
Steve & Rhianne O'Rourke
Jeanny Wang
Phil Hoyle
Susie Templeton
Ricky Rew
Chris Baldwin
Emily Sharman
Ruth Spencer
Nazar & Jane Georgis
Dean Ayres
Pete & Julie Johnson
Katharine Reedy
Sheila Matthews
Tina Dunn
John & Olive Drane
Mike Rose
Christine Cattanach
Dave & Lou Baker
Nick Butler
Sophia & Neil Popham
Andy Meek
Lisa Andradez
Rob Schellert
Robert Suekarran
John Wheatley
Alison Boulton
Lucy Bolster
Sam Richards
Matt Freer
Nick White
David Webster
Sue Grant
Cathy & Steve Ross
Justin Duckworth
Marcus Giddy
Sarah Glasswell
Jenny Baker
James Fox Robinson
John Stephenson
Kerry Shipley
Sergey Kochergan
Dirk Kähler
Peter Norman
Johnny Douglas
Peter Carmody-Heaton
Dylan Barker
Edward Dickel
Tina Hodgett
Jonathan Rowe
Idina Dunmore

info@getsidetracked.co